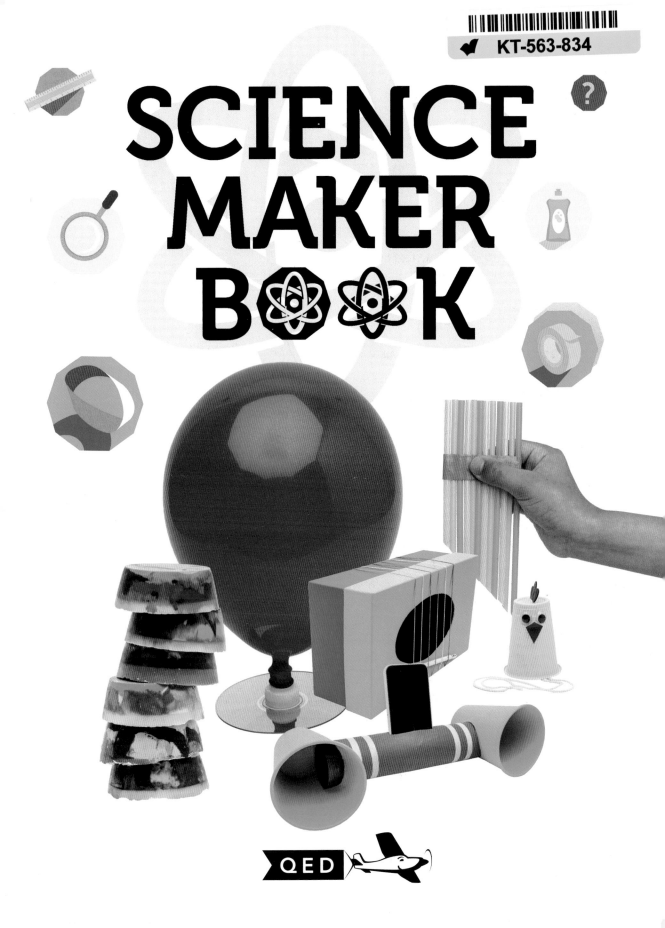

SCIENCE MAKER BOOK

QED

Contents

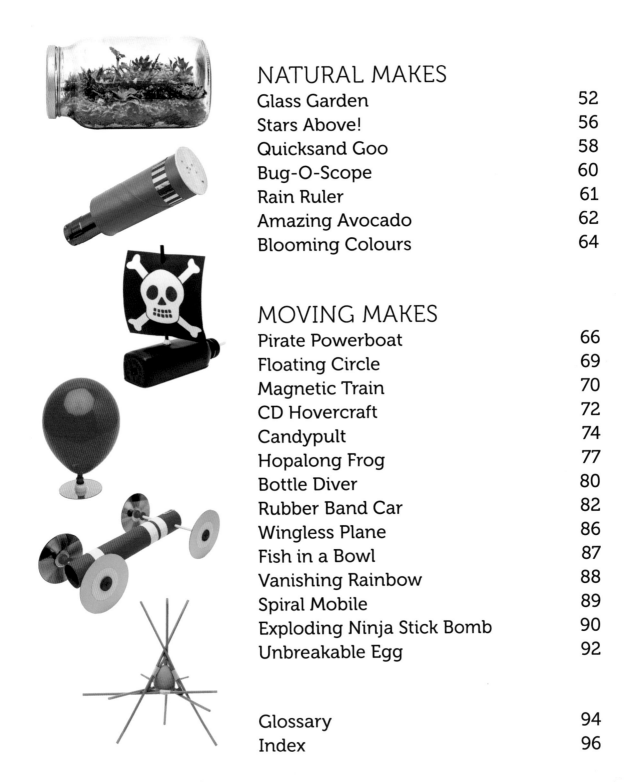

NATURAL MAKES

MOVING MAKES

Science Makes the World Go Round

Hi there, and welcome to the Science Maker book, your guide to a host of fun things you can make at home that rely on real science to make them work.

WELCOME ABOARD!

You're clearly a person of fine judgement – otherwise you wouldn't be holding this book – and so we're delighted that you've chosen to join us on this voyage of scientific discovery. Before we start, let's talk a bit about what you can look forward to in the pages that follow.

We've deliberately chosen a mix of 'makes' that demonstrate different scientific principles, so while you're having fun you can find out more about everything from Newton's Laws of Motion and **magnetic fields**, through to kinetic **energy** and surface tension.

7

Easy to follow step-by-step instructions lead you through each of the 'makes'.

YOU WILL NEED

'You Will Need' panels show you what tools and materials to assemble for each project.

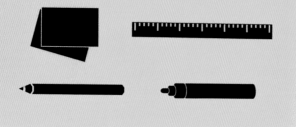

EVERYDAY ITEMS

Science affects every part of our lives, whether we realise it or not, and that's why we've chosen to make most of our projects with things you can find around the house. Sure, there are one or two projects where you might need to buy items – powerful magnets or wooden dowels – but they're all readily available online at low cost; and we think that once you see the results you'll agree it was money well spent.

We've also worked hard to make sure that some of our 'makes' can be made in minutes, while others will take more time – and effort. (Hey, science should be fun, not necessarily easy!)

Warning:
You should be able to complete almost all of the projects on your own, but if we think adult supervision is necessary, we'll tell you. Watch out for 'Warning' alerts that tell you when to ask for help.

THE SCIENCE:

Each project includes a panel that explains the science behind the project.

EXPERIMENT

The author and scientist Jules Verne once said: "Science is made up of mistakes, but they are mistakes that it is useful to make, because they lead little by little to the truth." So in the spirit of Monsieur Verne, we encourage you to make mistakes, to explore, to experiment and to think about the principles behind each project that you make, because as you'll discover, putting science to practical use is fantastic fun.

Enough of all this. We'll see you over the page…!

Paper Stairs

With just a sheet of paper, a pencil and a felt-tip pen you can create a set of steps that disappear down through the paper and into darkness...

YOU WILL NEED

White paper

Ruler

Pencil – a 2B is probably best

Black felt-tip or marker pen

1
Draw a rectangle on your piece of paper.

2
Next, draw vertical lines so they divide the rectangle as shown.

3
Starting at the top left-hand corner, draw a 45 degree line, then a straight line. Repeat until you reach the right-hand edge of the paper.

4
Go over the lines you have just drawn with a marker pen. Then go over the two edges shown.

5
Colour in the shape with the marker pen. Then, using the pencil, fill in the thin vertical blocks.

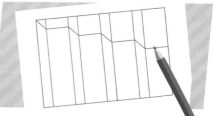

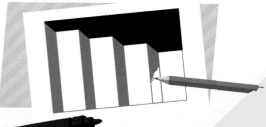

6

Measure halfway down the right-hand side of the drawing and draw a light pencil line from this point across to the top left-hand corner. Shade this area in lightly.

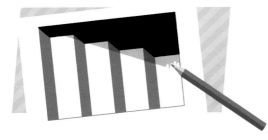

7

Finish off the shading and your **3-D** drawing is complete!

THE SCIENCE:
OPTICAL ILLUSION

Your brain has a lot more to do with what you see than you probably think it does. For example, your eyes actually see everything upside down, but your brain turns the images the right way up. Optical illusions work because your brain is always trying to make sense of what you're seeing. Every day you see thousands, probably millions, of different objects, and your brain has to work hard to keep up. In the stairs drawing below, the lines and shading create an illusion of a real set of stairs disappearing down into the paper. This illusion fools your brain into thinking the stairs have depth and are solid.

To see the 3-D effect even more clearly, try squeezing your eyes a little so they're nearly shut.

Soften the shadow effect by rubbing it gently with your finger.

Invisible Ink

Here's how to draw or write a message that no-one else can see – unless they know the secret of how to reveal it!

YOU WILL NEED

Half a lemon

Small bowl

Teaspoon

Water

Cotton bud

Piece of white paper

Lamp with light bulb (but not an energy-saving bulb)

1
Squeeze the juice of half a lemon into a small bowl.

2
Add two teaspoons of water to the lemon juice and stir with a cotton bud. Then use the cotton bud to draw or write your secret message on a sheet of paper.

3
When the paper is dry, hold it carefully over a lamp – but don't hold it too close or it will scorch.

4
Move the paper over the lamp until the picture or message is revealed!

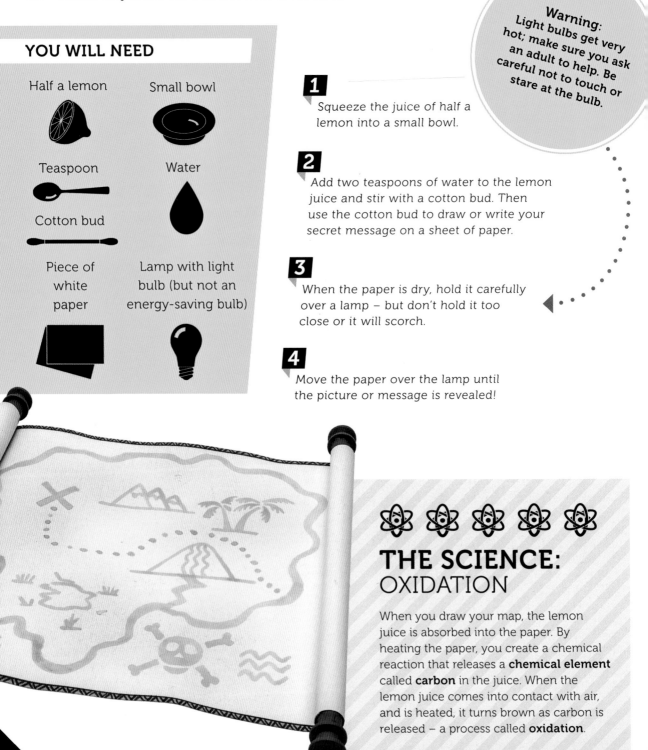

THE SCIENCE: OXIDATION

When you draw your map, the lemon juice is absorbed into the paper. By heating the paper, you create a chemical reaction that releases a **chemical element** called **carbon** in the juice. When the lemon juice comes into contact with air, and is heated, it turns brown as carbon is released – a process called **oxidation**.

Möbius Mystery

Cut a strip of paper in two, and you'll get two strips, right? Well...not always!
Amaze your friends with a Möbius strip, which only has one side!

YOU WILL NEED

Scissors   A sheet of
               thick paper or
               thin card

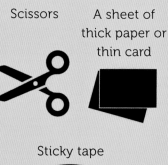

Sticky tape

Pencil

1 Cut a strip about 2 cm wide from the side of your sheet of paper or card.

2 Bend the ends of your strip over to make a loop, then twist one of the ends 180 degrees.

3 Tape the ends of the strip together. You've made a loop with a twist in it, called a Möbius strip.

4 Draw a line all the way along the middle of the strip until you're back to where you started. What happens?

5 Now for the really weird part. Carefully stick your scissors into the middle of the strip, and cut all the way along the line you drew. The result may not be quite what you expected!

For a little more magic, put two twists into the end before sticking the loop. Then cut along the middle and see what happens!

THE SCIENCE:
ONLY ONE SIDE, ONE EDGE

Because of the twist, a Möbius strip only has one side and one edge, not two. And that means it can't be cut in half!

Fish Wallpaper

You wouldn't want to wallpaper your bedroom with real fish, but these paper ones show how arranging a simple shape can produce some amazing, eye-boggling patterns.

YOU WILL NEED

Piece of paper

Ruler

Patience!

Pencil

1

Here's how we made our fish. Start by drawing a vertical line, 2.5 cm long.

2

Next, measure 2.5 cm horizontally from the top and bottom of the vertical line and mark two dots.

Why patience? Because to create proper tessellations you're going to need lots of fish! You could either copy your design one at a time (get your friends to help) or make a card template and draw around it lots of times.

This tessellation uses a simple nose-to-nose pattern.

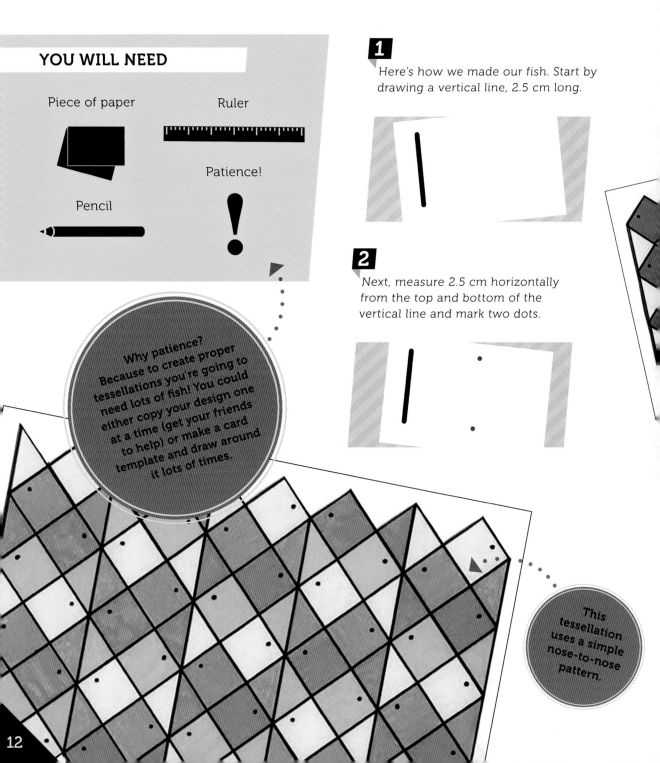

3

Join the top of the vertical line to the bottom dot and the bottom of the vertical line to the top dot.

4

Next, from the point where the two lines cross over, measure 2.5 cm to the right. Mark a dot there.

5

Join the two 'hanging' lines to the dot, then add a final dot for an eye. Choose a pattern and repeat your fish design lots of times.

Here the fish are stacked on top of each other facing first left and then right to create the pattern.

THE SCIENCE: TESSELLATION

Tessellation is a type of **geometry**. Its two most common rules are 1) there must not be any gaps between the shapes and 2) the corner of one shape cannot lie alongside the side of another shape. The easiest shapes to tessellate are triangles, squares and hexagons. Our fish is made up of a triangle and a square, and as you can see, you can create different tessellations by arranging the fish in various ways.

The fish in this pattern are nose-to-nose but staggered to the right to form an entirely different tessellation.

13

Recycled Crayons

Got loads of broken old crayons? We'll show you how to give them a new lease of life.

YOU WILL NEED

Old broken wax crayons

Silicon baking tray (the rubbery kind)

Oven

1

Take your crayons, peel off the paper wrappers and break them into the moulds.

2

Make sure you mix up the colours for a more interesting effect.

3

Pre-heat the oven to 90°C and ask an adult to pop the tray in. Leave it for about 10 to 15 minutes.

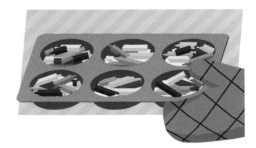

4

Check on the tray. Hopefully the crayons will have melted into a colourful liquid.

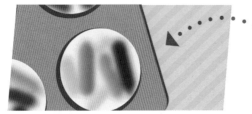

You may be tempted to see if the crayons will melt in the sun. Don't waste your time. It won't be hot enough.

14

5

Wait for the liquid to cool, then tip your crayon discs out of the tray. The flat sides are great for colouring large areas quickly. The tops are good for doing leaf rubbings, and you can get thin lines by using the edges – turn the disc slightly to change colour!

THE SCIENCE:
PHASES OF MATTER

Matter is everything you see around you. It is almost always either a solid, a liquid or a gas – these are its 'phases' or 'states'. By heating matter, you can change its state from one form to another. If you could peer inside a solid object, you'd see that it was made of tiny **particles** held together by **forces**. When you heat the object, these forces are no longer strong enough to hold the particles together and the object melts. Let it cool and the forces are strong enough to hold the particles together again to make a solid. The crayons start out as solid, heat melts them into a liquid, then they return to their solid state as they cool.

Crafty Compass

Find out where you are the old-fashioned way, by making a compass that magically (or should we say 'magnetically'?) always points north.

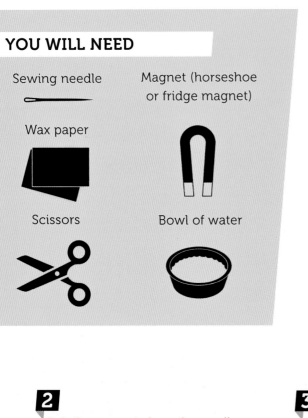

YOU WILL NEED

Sewing needle

Magnet (horseshoe or fridge magnet)

Wax paper

Scissors

Bowl of water

The stronger the magnet you use, the longer the needle will stay magnetised and the better your compass will work. You could try ceramic disc magnets like those used on fridge magnets.

1
Take a needle – careful, it's sharp! – and a magnet.

2
Rub the magnet along the needle 20 times – always in the same direction – starting at the eye and moving towards the point.

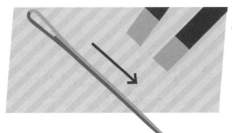

3
Put the magnet and needle to one side. Now take a sheet of wax paper.

Keep all magnets away from computers and mobile phones. They can mess them up and could even stop them from working.

4

Cut out a circle of wax paper, making sure that its diameter is shorter than the length of the needle.

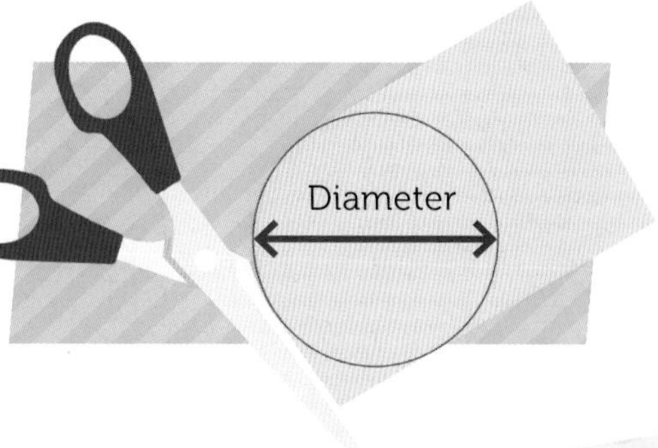

Diameter

5

Poke the point of the needle through the wax paper circle.

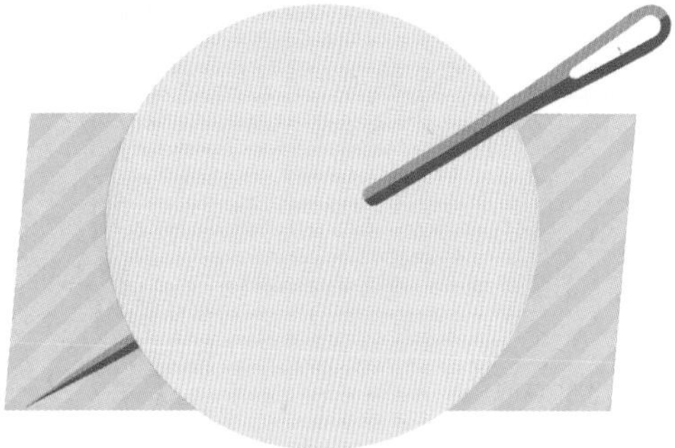

S

W

E

N

You can decorate your bowl with a cardboard rim. When the needle stops moving, add the compass points N (north), E (east), S (south) and W (west) using the sun as your guide (see page 18).

CONTINUED...

6

Push the tip of the needle back through the paper. You want the needle to sit centrally on the paper.

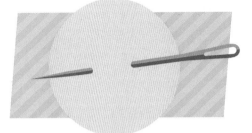

7

Take your bowl of water and place the needle and wax paper carefully onto the surface of the water.

8

After a moment, the needle will start to move all by itself. When it stops, it will be lined up with north and south.

Compasses are still used today, especially by hikers far from a mobile phone signal. Luckily, they can rely on this two-thousand-year-old technology to find out which way to go!

THE SCIENCE:
MAGNETIC ATTRACTION

When you rubbed the magnet along the needle, you turned the needle into a magnet. How? Well, normally metal objects have tiny bits of magnetic stuff inside them that push and pull in different directions. By dragging the magnet along the needle, you made all these magnetic bits face the same way, giving the needle a magnetic direction.

Planet Earth is itself a gigantic magnet, and because magnets either attract or repel each other, one end of the magnetised needle will be attracted to Earth's magnetic north pole and the other to the magnetic south pole. You can work out which end of the needle is pointing north by taking your compass outside on a sunny morning. The sun rises in the east, so from that you can easily see which way is north.

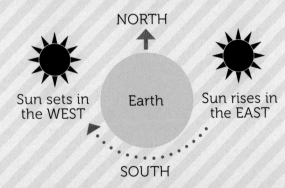

NORTH

Sun sets in the WEST

Earth

Sun rises in the EAST

SOUTH

Secret Jewellery

Imagine a necklace or wristband that displays a secret word that only you can read. It's easy to make one, so long as you can think like a computer!

YOU WILL NEED

Lots of beads, but only two colours

A length of elastic cord or a waxed cotton cord

> You don't have to use beads; you can use anything that can be threaded onto cord so long as there are only two types, representing 0 and 1.

1

Start by deciding on the word you want to hide in your jewellery and divide your beads into two piles. The blue beads are 0s and the orange beads are 1s.

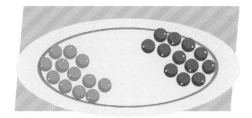

2

Using the **Binary** Code alphabet table on page 20, create the first letter of your secret word. Our word is the name 'Rob', so we'll start with 'R'.

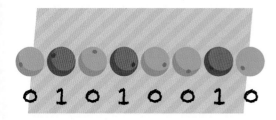

0 1 0 1 0 0 1 0

CONTINUED...

3

Now make the next letter. Ours is 'o'.

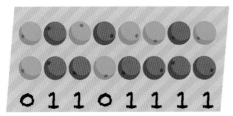

o 1 1 o 1 1 1 1

4

Our last letter is 'b'. Carry on until you have all the letters you need.

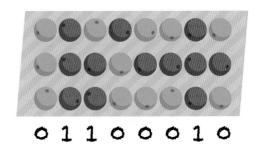

o 1 1 o o o 1 o

5

Next, string the first letter onto the cord.

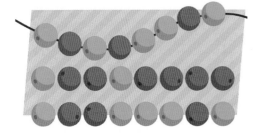

6

String your other letters, then cut the cord to length and knot each end.

BINARY CODE ALPHABET TABLE

Capital letters	Binary code	Capital letters	Binary code	Small letters	Binary code	Small letters	Binary code
A	01000001	N	01001110	a	01100001	n	01101110
B	01000010	O	01001111	b	01100010	o	01101111
C	01000011	P	01010000	c	01100011	p	01110000
D	01000100	Q	01010001	d	01100100	q	01110001
E	01000101	R	01010010	e	01100101	r	01110010
F	01000110	S	01010011	f	01100110	s	01110011
G	01000111	T	01010100	g	01100111	t	01110100
H	01001000	U	01010101	h	01101000	u	01110101
I	01001001	V	01010110	i	01101001	v	01110110
J	01001010	W	01010111	j	01101010	w	01110111
K	01001011	X	01011000	k	01101011	x	01111000
L	01001100	Y	01011001	l	01101100	y	01111001
M	01001101	Z	01011010	m	01101101	z	01111010

Now read THE SCIENCE to understand the logic behind turning letters into 0s and 1s.

⚛ ⚛ ⚛ ⚛ ⚛
THE SCIENCE:
BINARY CODE

When a computer 'sees' a letter, it actually sees eight empty slots into which it puts either a 0 or a 1, because that's all it understands. Each slot represents a number: slot 1 has a value of 128, slot 2 is 64, slot 3 is 32, slot 4 is 16, slot 5 is 8, slot 6 is 4, slot 7 is 2 and slot 8 is 1.

OK, so how do we turn the letter 'A' into 01000001? Start by getting the letter's ascii number from the Number Code table below (A = 65). Now, remember the values of your eight empty slots? To make 65, you need one lot of 64 (so we put a 1 in slot 2) plus one lot of 1 (so we put a 1 in slot 8). All the other slots will contain a 0.

Capital 'A' = ascii number 65

Slot	1	2	3	4	5	6	7	8
Value	128	64	32	16	8	4	2	1
Binary code	0	1	0	0	0	0	0	1

See if you can work out the binary code for the letter 'd'. First, find its ascii number from the Number Code table below. Then work out which value numbers will add together to equal that ascii number. You can check your answer by looking up 'd' in the Binary Code alphabet table on page 20.

Small 'd' = ascii number ?

Slot	1	2	3	4	5	6	7	8
Value	128	64	32	16	8	4	2	1
Binary code	?	?	?	?	?	?	?	?

NUMBER CODE

Capital letters	ascii number	Small letters	ascii number
A	65	a	97
B	66	b	98
C	67	c	99
D	68	d	100
E	69	e	101
F	70	f	102
G	71	g	103
H	72	h	104
I	73	i	105
J	74	j	106
K	75	k	107
L	76	l	108
M	77	m	109
N	78	n	110
O	79	o	111
P	80	p	112
Q	81	q	113
R	82	r	114
S	83	s	115
T	84	t	116
U	85	u	117
V	86	v	118
W	87	w	119
X	88	x	120
Y	89	y	121
Z	90	z	122

Remember to put your jewellery on the right way round, otherwise your code won't make sense!

Coded Messages

The code wheel has been helping people send secret messages for more than two thousand years. Now it's your turn!

YOU WILL NEED

Compass   Thin card   Protractor   Glue stick   Felt pens   Adhesive putty

Scissors

Pencil   Ruler   Paper fastener

1

Using a compass and pencil, draw a 15-cm-diameter and a 13-cm-diameter circle on some paper or thin card. Use a protractor and ruler to divide each circle into 26 segments.

> A circle is 360 degrees. To divide it into 26 almost equal parts, you'll need 22 segments of 14 degrees and four segments of 13 degrees.

2

If you've drawn your circles on paper, cut them out and stick them onto some card. Colour the segments.

3

Next, add the letters of the alphabet in order around both discs, like this.

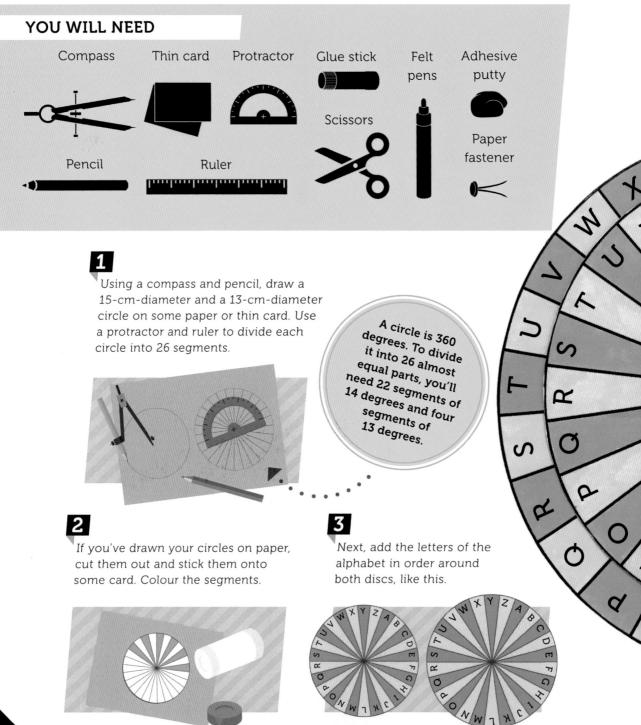

4

Place the small disc on top of the larger one and centre them over a lump of adhesive putty. Push a sharp pencil through the centres into the putty to make a hole, then join the discs together with a paper fastener.

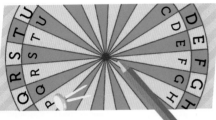

5

Here's your finished code wheel. So how does it work?

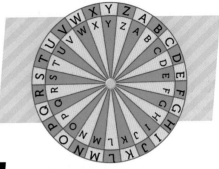

6

It's simple! Both you and the person you're swapping messages with need a code wheel. Before you start, agree how many letters to move the inner wheel to the right or left to create your code. We've moved it two places to the right, so the inner 'A' lines up with the outer 'C'. Now read THE SCIENCE to find out how to write your message.

THE SCIENCE:
SUBSTITUTION CODE

This simple code is hard to break. Find the first letter of your message in the outer circle, and write down the corresponding letter in the inner circle. For example, if your message is 'SEND HELP', instead of S write Q, instead of E write C, and so on. It should look like this:

```
S E N D   H E L P
Q C L B   F C J N
```

By sending the message QCLB FCJN, anyone who doesn't know the code will never know what's going on!

Heavenly Music

OK, so maybe it's not going to make you sound like an angel, but our shoebox harp can carry a simple tune and is great fun to make.

YOU WILL NEED

Pencil

Shoebox

Scissors

Rubber bands

1

Mark a point roughly at the centre of the shoebox lid, then use your pencil to make a hole there.

2

Next, draw an oval shape around the hole.

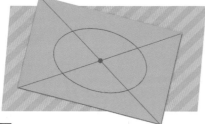

3

Poke your scissors through the hole and begin to cut out the oval.

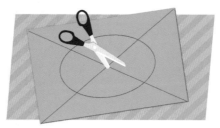

4

You can start by cutting out the oval shape roughly. Then when you reach the line you have drawn, cut along it as neatly as you can.

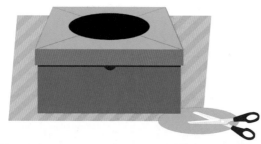

5

Stretch a rubber band around the shoebox and slide it over the hole. Add more rubber bands.

6

Finally, carefully slide the pencil under the strings and angle it slightly as shown in the picture. You're ready to join the heavenly choir!

Be careful when you're stretching the rubber bands over the box. If one snaps and hits you, it's going to sting.

THE SCIENCE:
VIBRATIONS

Stringed instruments make a sound when their strings vibrate; that's why you need to pluck the strings of a harp to hear notes. The strings make different notes depending on their thickness, the amount of tension they're under (how tight they are) and their length. The sound hole in the harp helps to make the sound louder by **amplifying** the **vibrations** and allowing the top of the shoebox to vibrate slightly. The pencil raises the strings off the lid so they can vibrate more freely.

The Pipes of Pan

To make this musical instrument, all you need are a few drinking straws and some tape. Getting a real tune out of it may take some practice though!

YOU WILL NEED

Sticky tape   Scissors

Drinking straws

1
Unwind a length of sticky tape and lay the drinking straws across it. Try to line up the ends as neatly as you can.

2
When you've got all the straws in place, cut the tape and wrap the ends across the straws to keep them in place.

3
Cut across the straws at an angle so that each straw is a different length.

4
Hold your panpipes up to your mouth and blow across the top of each straw to make different notes.

THE SCIENCE:
PITCH

Blowing across the top of a straw makes the air inside vibrate, which in turn produces a note. Long straws make notes with a low **pitch** and short straws make higher-pitched notes. If all the straws were the same length, they'd all produce the same note.

Panpipes are usually closed pipes. Try blocking the bottom of your straws with tiny blobs of plasticine to play lower and clearer notes.

Smartphone Boom Box

Why put up with tinny sound from your smartphone when you could turn it into a bass-blasting boom box?

If you're not getting a good sound, make sure you've put the right end of the phone inside the boom box.

YOU WILL NEED

Smartphone

Cardboard tube from kitchen roll

Marker pen

Scissors

Two paper cups

1

Hold your smartphone midway along the cardboard tube and draw around its base. Carefully cut out the shape with scissors.

2

Place one end of the cardboard tube against the side of one of the paper cups and draw around it.

3
Cut out the circle you've just drawn on the cup, then push the cup onto the end of the cardboard tube.

4
Repeat with the other end of the tube.

5
Play some music and pop your smartphone into the slot, making sure that the speaker is inside the cardboard tube. **Boom!** Your music will now be much louder.

THE SCIENCE:
DIRECTIONAL SOUND

By placing the speaker inside the tube, you're giving the sound waves a space to **resonate** and become amplified. Channelling them out through the cups makes the music sound much louder.

27

Ring Them Bells

Tap a coat hanger against a hard surface and it makes a dull 'ting' – but here's how to turn it into a beautiful bell with just a couple of bits of string!

YOU WILL NEED

Metal coat hanger
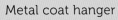

A handy door

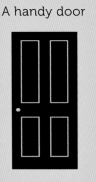

String, two long pieces both the same length

1

Take your first piece of string and tie it to one of the corners of the metal coat hanger.

3

Find a door and stand sideways on to it. Hold the coat hanger in front of you by the two bits of string and swing it against the door. Hmm, that little 'ting' isn't very exciting, is it?

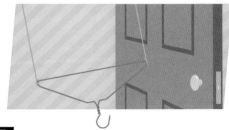

2

Then do exactly the same on the other corner with the other piece of string.

4

Let's try again. This time, wrap the string around each forefinger.

5

Then gently put your two forefingers into your ears.

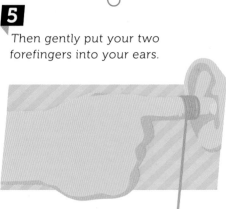

6

Swing the coat hanger against the door again and you'll hear the sound of a ringing bell!

You can also try getting a friend to hit the coat hanger with a metal spoon. You'll hear a bright, loud clang!

THE SCIENCE:
CONDUCTING SOUND

When we hear something, it's because there are vibrations creating sound waves, which travel through the air. Now, air is good at conducting sound, but string is much better because it's a solid. (Water is also a good sound conductor, which is why things sound booming under water). The sound waves from the hanger spread out through the air in all directions and so not much sound reaches your ear. By wrapping the string around your fingers and putting your fingers very gently into your ears, much more of the sound can reach your ears. The sound waves travel from the coat hanger up the string and directly into your ears, and this transforms the weedy 'ting' into a booming 'bong'.

Playin' the Blues

Feeling fed up? If you've got the blues inside and want to get them out then there's only one instrument for you: the harmonica.

YOU WILL NEED

Plastic straw

Scissors

One large rubber band

Two lollysticks or craft sticks, the same size

Two small rubber bands

If you can't find any small rubber bands, just make sure they're thin and wrap them around the sticks lots of times. It'll have the same effect.

1

Cut two short lengths from the plastic straw; they need to be slightly longer than the lollysticks are wide.

2

Take the large rubber band and wrap it lengthways around one of the lollysticks.

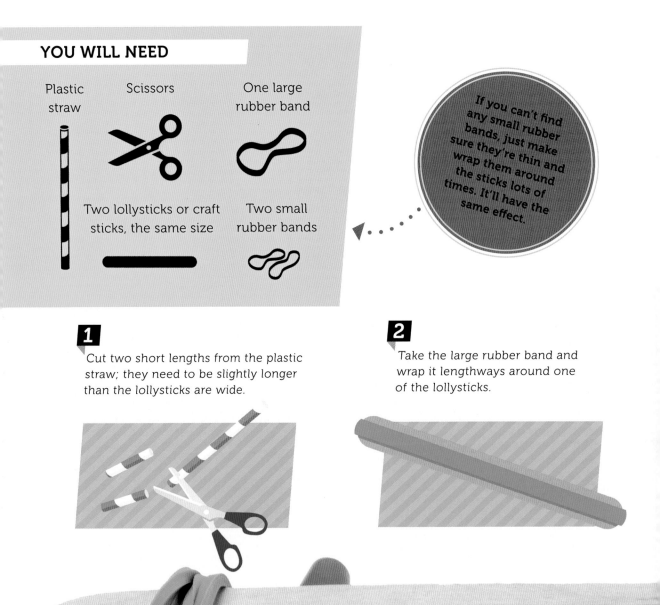

3

Slide the two pieces of straw under the rubber band at either end of the lollystick.

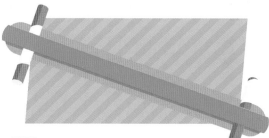

4

Place the second lollystick on top of the first one so they line up.

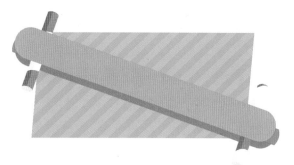

5

Wrap one of the small rubber bands around one end of the two lollysticks.

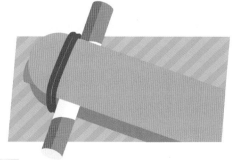

6

Repeat step 5 at the other end. Now blow between the lollysticks to start playing the blues!

THE SCIENCE: FREQUENCY AND PITCH

When you blow into the harmonica, the rubber band between the lollysticks vibrates and generates a sound. Moving the two cut straws closer together will alter the **frequency** at which the rubber band vibrates and make the pitch or note higher. Move the straws back towards the ends and the pitch becomes lower again.

You can also change the pitch by blowing more softly or blowing harder; both will change the frequency at which the rubber band vibrates and move the note up or down the musical scale.

Clucking Cup

How is it possible to make a plastic cup cluck like a chicken? It's actually easier than you think, and it really does sound like a chicken!

YOU WILL NEED

Sharp pencil

Cotton (not nylon) string or wool

Marker pen

PVA glue

Scissors

Plastic cup, a yellow one works well

Red paper

Pair of googly eyes

1
Use a sharp pencil to poke two small holes in the bottom of the plastic cup.

2
Tie a knot at one end of the string. Thread the other end through both holes, then tie a knot in the end.

3
Fold the red paper in half and draw the chicken's comb and beak along the fold, as shown.

4
Cut out the comb following your pen line; don't cut along the fold. Glue along the fold and stick it to the cup.

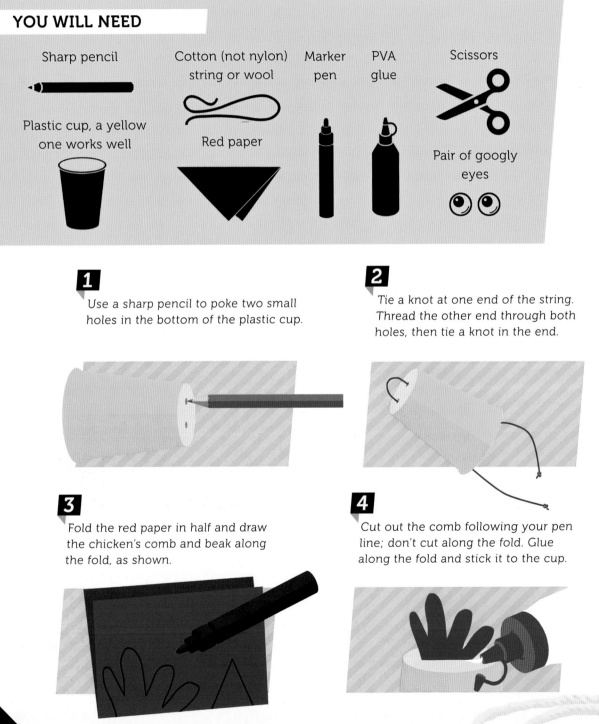

5

Cut out the beak in the same way, open it out and stick the fold to the front of the cup. Add two googly eyes.

6

Now, hold the cup up high in one hand, wet the fingers of your other hand, then pinch the string just below the cup and, gripping the string, jerk your hand down in small, sharp movements. You'll hear an incredibly realistic clucking sound, just like a real chicken!

If you're not getting a good sound, try holding a bit of wet sponge between your fingers and jerking that down the string.

THE SCIENCE:
SOUNDING BOARD

The vibrations of the string, caused by the movement of your fingers, travel along the string and are amplified by the hollow cup, which acts as a sounding board. (If you cover the open end of the cup, the vibrations from the string are almost silent = no sound). Pianos and guitars use wooden sounding boards to make their sounds louder in the same way.

Chocolate Pictures

Like water, chocolate can switch between solid and liquid, depending on the temperature. Unlike water, melted chocolate is delicious, so why not use it to make pictures and then turn them into cake decorations?

YOU WILL NEED

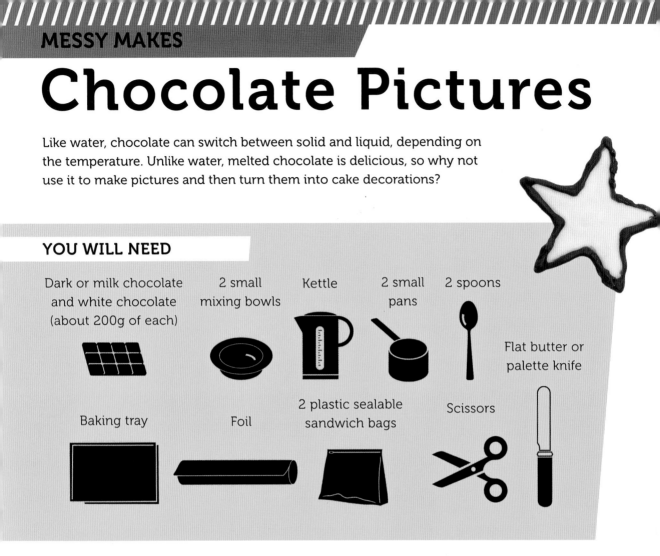

Dark or milk chocolate and white chocolate (about 200g of each)

2 small mixing bowls

Kettle

2 small pans

2 spoons

Flat butter or palette knife

Baking tray

Foil

2 plastic sealable sandwich bags

Scissors

1
Break the chocolate into two bowls.

2
Ask an adult to boil a kettle of water and then half-fill both the pans with the hot water. Put the bowls containing chocolate on top of each pan.

3
After five minutes the chocolate will slowly melt. Stir it gently with separate spoons.

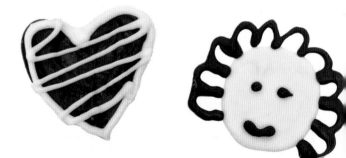

4

Cover the baking tray with smooth foil. Spoon the melted chocolate into the sandwich bags and seal them up.

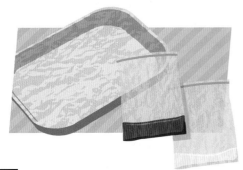

5

Squeeze each type of chocolate into the corner of its bag, then snip off the tip of the corner to make a hole. The hole should be as tiny as possible!

6

You can now use the bags like pens to draw pictures, letters or numbers on the foil. Keep them quite small.

7

Put your pictures in a cool place for about an hour. When they have set, lift them off the foil with a flat knife.

THE SCIENCE: MELTING AND 'FREEZING'

Chocolate melts (turns into a liquid) as it warms up, and 'freezes' (turns back into a solid) as it gets colder. That's because it's made of **molecules** that are always moving. When they get hotter, they move apart a little and can slide over each other, making a runny liquid. When they cool down, they move less and stick together. Chocolate melts at 35°C. It melts in your mouth because your body temperature is slightly warmer, at 37°C.

DIY Ice Cream

You probably hate ice cream, right? So you're probably not interested in finding out how to make it yourself in a bag? Thought so!

YOU WILL NEED

Old tablecloth

1 large sealable freezer bag

Lots of ice cubes (about 48)

Standard measuring cup (150g)

Salt, about 70 g

Measuring jug

Milk, 285 ml

Sugar, 2 tablespoons

Vanilla essence, half a teaspoon

One small sealable freezer bag

Medium-sized bowl

1
On an old tablecloth, half fill a large freezer bag with ice. Use a measuring cup to add the salt.

2
Pour the milk into the measuring jug, then add the sugar and vanilla essence.

3
Put the small freezer bag in a bowl (to prevent mess) and pour the milk mixture into the bag.

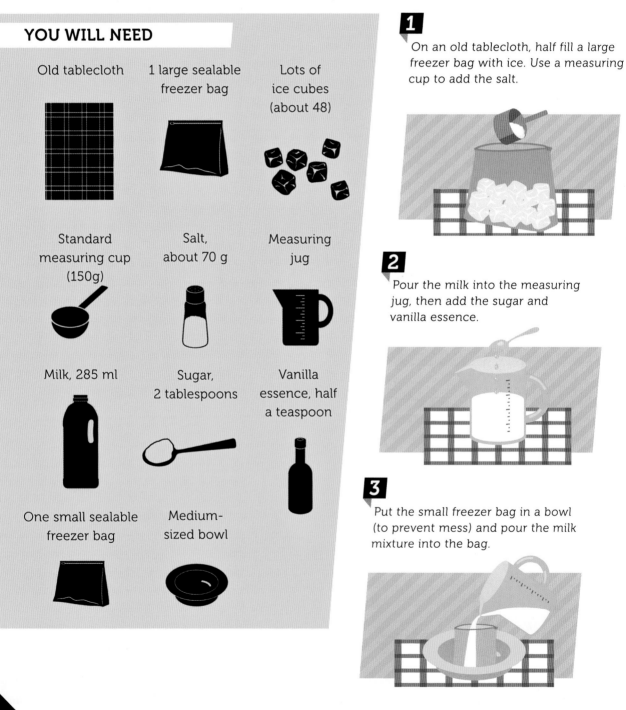

4

Carefully seal the small bag and then put it inside the large bag.

5

Make sure the large bag is sealed, then shake it for 10 minutes to make lovely thick ice cream.

THE SCIENCE:
TEMPERATURE

If you don't add salt to your ice, then your ice cream probably won't work because you won't be able to make it cold enough. Adding salt lowers the temperature at which the ice melts. As it melts, it draws heat out of the milk/sugar/vanilla mixture, causing it to freeze into ice cream!

If your ice cream isn't solidifying (and your arms are getting tired), try adding another tablespoon of salt to the bag of ice.

Fancy a different flavour? Just add a tablespoon of sifted cocoa powder to the mix to make chocolate ice cream.

Vinegar Volcano

It's time to unleash one of nature's most awe-inspiring spectacles: the mighty erupting volcano. Yes, it may be a pint-sized version, but it's brilliantly effective and dead easy to make.

YOU WILL NEED

Tablecloth or newspaper

Two empty bottles

Sticky tape

Square of thick card

Old newspaper

PVA glue

Bowl to mix glue in

Water

Paints

Funnel

White vinegar

Food colouring

Washing-up liquid

Measuring spoon

Baking soda (bicarbonate of soda), 60 g

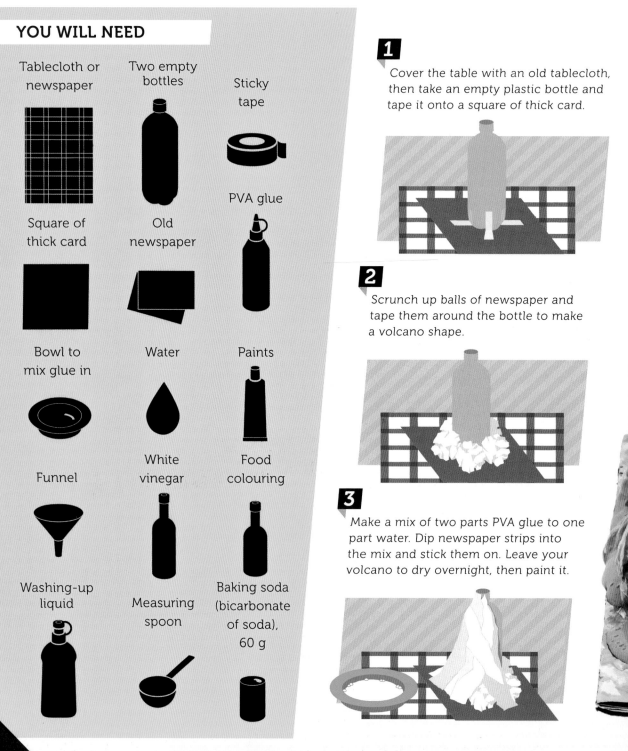

1
Cover the table with an old tablecloth, then take an empty plastic bottle and tape it onto a square of thick card.

2
Scrunch up balls of newspaper and tape them around the bottle to make a volcano shape.

3
Make a mix of two parts PVA glue to one part water. Dip newspaper strips into the mix and stick them on. Leave your volcano to dry overnight, then paint it.

4

Take the other empty bottle, pop the funnel in the top and fill the bottle one-third full with white vinegar.

5

Add a few drops of food colouring; red is good for dramatic lava.

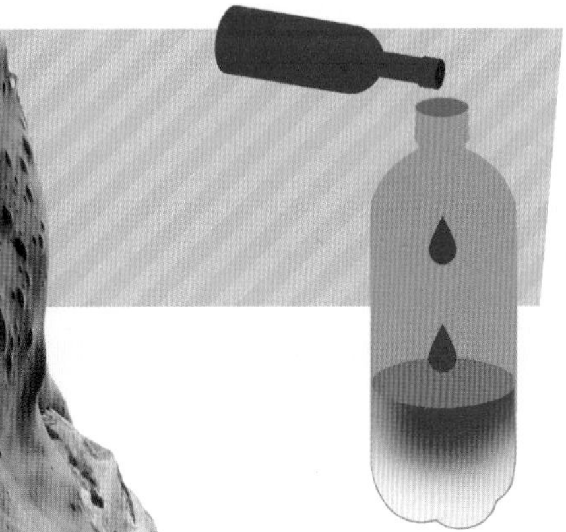

There are about 1500 active volcanoes in the world. Congratulations on making it 1501!

You could get your friends to help you paint and decorate your papier maché volcano.

CONTINUED...

6

Add a good squeeze of washing-up liquid to the coloured vinegar.

7

Now, using your measuring spoon and a dry funnel, tip the baking soda into the bottle inside the volcano.

8

Next, quite quickly start to pour the vinegar mixture into the bottle inside the volcano.

9

After a few seconds your volcano will erupt, spewing 'lava' everywhere!

THE SCIENCE:
ACID REACTION

The baking soda is a compound called sodium bicarbonate or bicarbonate of soda. The vinegar is an **acid**. When these two get together they react to produce carbon dioxide gas (hence all the bubbling!). Why the washing-up liquid? The detergent in the liquid helps to trap the bubbles created by the carbon dioxide, so you get much better 'lava' from your volcano.

Glow-in-the-Dark Jelly

This glowing dessert will be a real hit at Halloween, but you don't need to wait until then. Eat it with the lights off – and enjoy!

YOU WILL NEED

Measuring jug

Hot water, 285 ml (or half the water in the packet's instructions)

Tonic water, 285 ml (or same amount as hot water used)

Two clear plastic cups

Blacklight (also called a UV or ultraviolet light)

Jelly

Spoon

Mashed banana

Optional: sugar or chocolate sprinkles

Warning: Never look directly at UV light as it can cause serious damage to eyes. Adult supervision needed.

1

Separate the packet of jelly cubes into a measuring jug and ask an adult to add 285 ml of hot water (or half the water in the packet's instructions).

2

Give the mixture a good stir with a spoon. Keep stirring until the jelly has dissolved.

3

Next, add 285 ml of tonic water (or the same amount of tonic water as hot water that you added earlier).

4

Give the liquid another good stir to combine everything well and then pour the mixture into two clear plastic cups.

5

Put the cups of jelly in the fridge to set (check the packet's instructions to find out how long to leave them). When the jelly has set – check by giving the cups a bit of a wobble – spoon some mashed banana on top.

Don't like banana? No worries, you can use any fruit you do like, such as berries or a slice of kiwi fruit.

6

You may want to finish off by adding sprinkles. The sweetness will help to 'smooth out' the slightly sharp taste of the tonic water.

7

Finally, turn off the lights and turn on your blacklight. Shine it from behind the cups and you'll see your jelly spookily glowing in the dark. Best of all, you can eat the results!

THE SCIENCE:
FLUORESCENT SUBSTANCES AND ULTRAVIOLET LIGHT

OK, here's what's happening. All around us is something called the electromagnetic spectrum, a sort of super-highway of things we can see, such as visible light, and things that we can't, such as radio waves, microwaves and ultraviolet light. When you shine the blacklight (ultraviolet light) onto the jelly, you 'excite' a substance in the tonic water called quinine, and that's what glows. Quinine glows because it's fluorescent. It soaks up ultraviolet light, which is invisible to the human eye, and then discharges it (even in the dark) as the kind of normal light that we can see. When you turn the blacklight off, you'll notice that the cups stop glowing, because the reaction inside the jelly stops almost as soon as the light disappears.

Marble Dairy Butter

There's nothing quite like hot-freshly-buttered toast – and if you're prepared to roll up your sleeves, you can make your own butter!

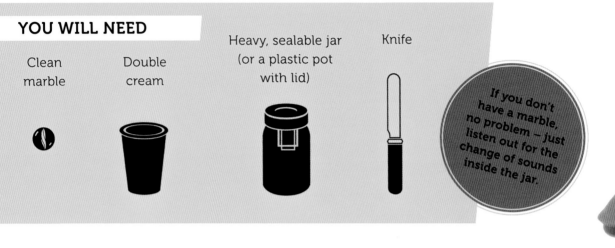

YOU WILL NEED

Clean marble

Double cream

Heavy, sealable jar (or a plastic pot with lid)

Knife

If you don't have a marble, no problem – just listen out for the change of sounds inside the jar.

1

Start by carefully dropping the marble into a heavy glass (or plastic) jar. Don't use a thin glass jar as the glass may crack.

2

Pour the double cream into the jar until the jar is about half or two-thirds full.

3

Close the lid tightly. Now start to shake the jar back and forth.

4

When the marble stops making a noise, you'll have extra thick cream, but not butter! Keep shaking until you hear watery **buttermilk** sloshing in the jar.

5

Pour away the buttermilk, then use a knife to scoop out some butter and spread it on some toast. Mmmm!

THE SCIENCE:
PROPERTIES OF EMULSION

Double cream is what scientists call an emulsion; little drops of one liquid float around inside drops of another liquid, and the two don't mix. In cream, the first drops are made of fat. When you shake the jar, you're basically banging these little drops of fat together. When they hit each other, they start to stick together, forming larger drops. These in turn hit other, larger drops, until eventually you end up with one big drop of fat – butter – plus some watery buttermilk.

Because your home-made butter contains no salt, additives or preservatives, it won't taste exactly like butter from the shops – and it will only keep for a few days, even in the fridge.

Perfect Pinch Pot

Always fancied yourself as a master craftsperson? Now's your chance to prove it by making this simple clay pot.

1

First, roll your polymer clay into a ball using the palms of both hands. Since it'll be a small pot – maybe to hold keys or coins – it should sit in the palm of your hand like this.

2

Next, press your thumb into the centre of the ball, but don't push all the way through or you'll end up with a doughnut!

3

Now use both thumbs to widen the hole you just made.

4

Continue working the clay until it resembles a bowl.

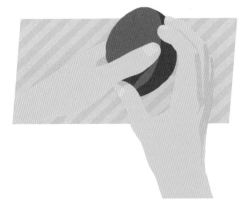

5

Leave the bowl to dry for two hours until it becomes leathery, but can still be shaped. Then smooth out any bumps with your fingers.

6

Now leave the bowl to dry completely until it feels cold and chalky to touch.

Check the instructions on your pack of polymer clay – drying times and oven temperatures may vary.

7

Preheat the oven to 135°C. Put the pot on a baking tray and ask an adult to pop it in the oven. Bake it for about 20 minutes per 6 mm of thickness.

8

Ask an adult to take the pot out of the oven. Leave it to cool, then paint it. When dry, seal it with PVA glue mixed with a drop of water.

Polymer clay has tiny holes in the surface. **Bacteria** can breed in these holes, so this bowl isn't for eating or drinking out of.

THE SCIENCE:
EVAPORATION

'Real' clay is made up of tiny particles of stuff (called aluminium silicate) mixed with water. Heating clay to 500°C drives water from the clay (it **evaporates**) and the particles join together strongly. The clay shrinks a little and becomes pottery. Polymer clay is made of tiny bits of polyvinyl chloride (PVC) mixed with **plasticizer**, which makes it flexible. Putting the polymer clay in the oven makes the plasticizer change and join the bits of PVC together strongly so the clay hardens.

Bubbleapalooza!

Blowing little bubbles is easy and – it turns out – blowing mega-bubbles is just as easy, thanks to this amazing giant bubble wand.

YOU WILL NEED

String, about 2 m long	Two wooden spoons with holes in the handles	Key	Washing-up bowl full of soapy water

1

Thread one end of the string through the hole in the handle of a wooden spoon and tie it off.

2

Next, thread the other end of the string through the hole in the key.

3

Pull the key down the string until it's about one third of the way along.

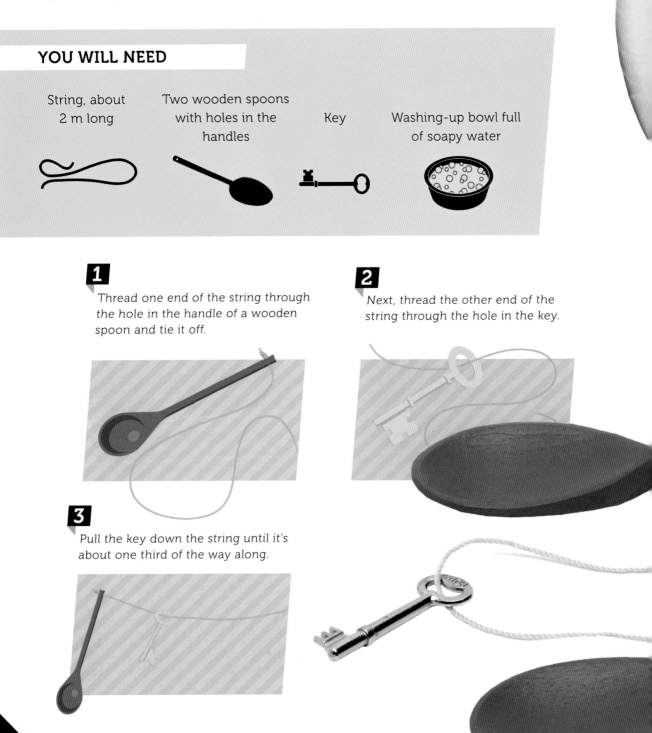

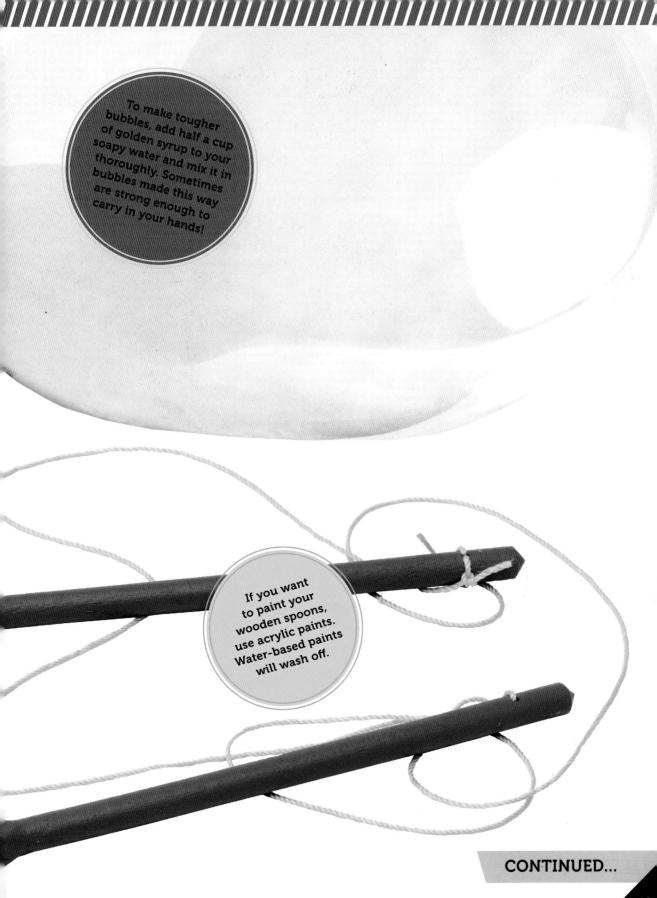

To make tougher bubbles, add half a cup of golden syrup to your soapy water and mix it in thoroughly. Sometimes bubbles made this way are strong enough to carry in your hands!

If you want to paint your wooden spoons, use acrylic paints. Water-based paints will wash off.

CONTINUED...

4

Take the loose end of the string and thread it through the second spoon handle. Pull this spoon about two thirds of the way along the string.

5

Tie the string around the handle of the second spoon. Hold both spoons up. The string should make a 'V' shape, with the key at the bottom.

6

About one third of the string will be dangling from the second handle. Take the end and tie it around the handle of the first spoon.

7

When you've finished the final knot, hold the wand out in front of you. The string should form a neat triangle.

Try making a square wand out of soft wire or pipe cleaners. Dip it in soapy water and blow. Will the bubbles be square or round? Believe it or not, as soon as a bubble forms, it'll turn into a perfect sphere – just like bubbles always do!

8

Take the wand outside and dip the key, string and spoon handles into soapy water a few times.

9

Now slowly walk backwards to make really massive bubbles – or forwards for slightly smaller ones – holding the wand out in front of you.

THE SCIENCE:
SURFACE TENSION

On its own, water has some surface tension – enough to let some insects walk across it – but not enough to form bubbles. Adding soap increases the surface tension and makes the water more 'elastic' so that bubbles can form, trapping air inside. A bubble always tries to take up the smallest amount of space it can while still holding all the air inside it, so the natural shape of a bubble is a sphere.

Glass Garden

Did you know that you can put plants and soil into a jar and seal it up, and your glass garden will continue to grow? Here's how to make one.

YOU WILL NEED

Glass jar between 1 and 3 litres

Cardboard box

Trowel

Soil

Small, non-flowering plants and moss

Pieces of wood

Spoon

Water sprayer

Tweezers

Small stones

1
Find a large, clean glass jar with a sealable lid, such as a mason jar, or try a large pickle jar.

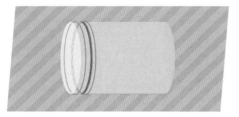

2
Take your box to a wooded area and use a trowel to collect some soil.

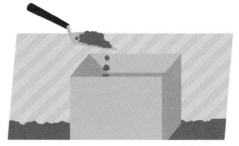

Unless you're with an adult who knows what they're doing, it's best not to pick wild plants in case they're protected under the law or are poisonous.

PLANTS THAT DO WELL

Choose woodland plants that need light but not direct sunlight. Small, slow-growing plants are best. Flowering plants don't do so well.

3

Collect some small plants from your garden (or you can buy some). Make sure you dig up their roots.

Spider ferns
Ivy
Maidenhair fern
Moss
Starfish plant
Nerve plant
Aquamarine

Golden clubmoss
Helexine (Baby's Tears)
'Moon Valley' friendship plant
Creeping Fig
Begonia rex

CONTINUED...

4

Choose different varieties to make your garden more interesting (see page 53).

5

Moss will do well in your garden, so don't forget to collect some.

6

Finally, find one or two small pieces of fallen wood to add variety.

7

Rinse the jar with water, then dry it well.

8

Keeping your jar on its side, cover the bottom with small stones.

9

Sprinkle some soil over the stones; remember to always wash hands after handling soil.

Putting stones at the bottom of the jar will improve drainage and help to keep your plants healthy.

10

Give your plants and wood a spray of water to dampen them.

11

Put your pieces of wood in the jar, then, using tweezers, start to place your plants on top of the soil.

12

When you've finished arranging your plants, close the lid. Put the jar in a well-lit area – but not in direct sunlight or it will get too hot – and your glass garden is complete!

THE SCIENCE:
TERRARIUM

A glass garden is called a terrarium – a sealed environment that is able to look after itself, a bit like a miniature planet Earth. The plants, and even the soil, release water vapour, which **condenses** and collects on the glass. The water droplets then trickle down the sides of the jar and go back into the soil. It's pretty much the same water cycle that happens outside in the real world.

During the day the plants take in light and carbon dioxide, and produce oxygen by photosynthesis. At night, when it's dark, they respire, taking the oxygen back in and producing carbon dioxide, so keeping your glass garden healthy.

Stars Above!

This simple 'make' will allow you to enjoy a starry night from the comfort of your own bed!

YOU WILL NEED

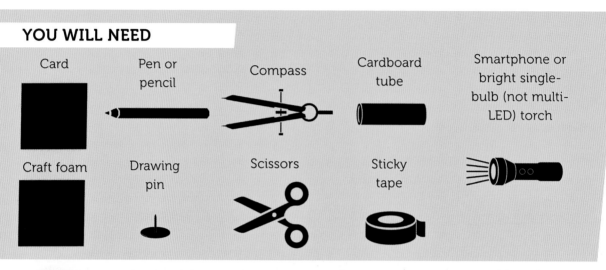

Card

Pen or pencil

Compass

Cardboard tube

Smartphone or bright single-bulb (not multi-LED) torch

Craft foam

Drawing pin

Scissors

Sticky tape

1

Draw 16 circles on some card. Make the circles slightly bigger than the end of the cardboard tube.

2

Next, copy the **constellations** onto the circles. Write the constellation names on the backs of the circles.

3

Place the card on some craft foam and stick a drawing pin through each dot.

Ursa Major the Great Bear	Scorpius the Scorpion	Orion the Hunter	Taurus the Bull	Pegasus the Flying Horse	Ursa Minor the Little Bear	Cassiopeia the Queen	Pisces the Fish

4

Cut out the circles. Hold one against the end of the tube with the name facing out, and attach it with sticky tape.

5

Tape the other end of the tube over your smartphone light or torch. Now shine it against a wall to see the stars.

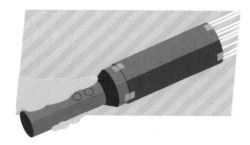

6

For best results, turn off the lights, draw the curtains and project the stars onto your bedroom ceiling.

THE SCIENCE:
CONSTELLATIONS

Astronomy is the study of objects in the sky such as planets, moons and stars. It has been studied for thousands of years. Constellations are an important part of astronomy; there are 88 in all. You'll only be able to see some of them at any one time, and you can only see some from the Southern Hemisphere.

| Leo
the Lion | Sagittarius
the Archer | Gemini
the Twins | Bootes
the Herdsman | Cygnus
the Swan | Perseus | Canis Major
the Big Dog | Hercules |

Quicksand Goo

Is it a solid? Is it a liquid? Is it both? Whatever it is, you'll find Quicksand Goo quite amazing to handle!

If you want to make creepy Quicksand Goo for Halloween, use black food colouring! Then get your friends to dip their hands in it and see what happens!

YOU WILL NEED

Packet of cornflour	Large bowl	Water (half as much as the dry cornflour)	Yellow food colouring

Scissors (optional)	Sticky tape (optional)	Foam craft sheet (optional)

1

Start by pouring a packet of cornflour into a bowl.

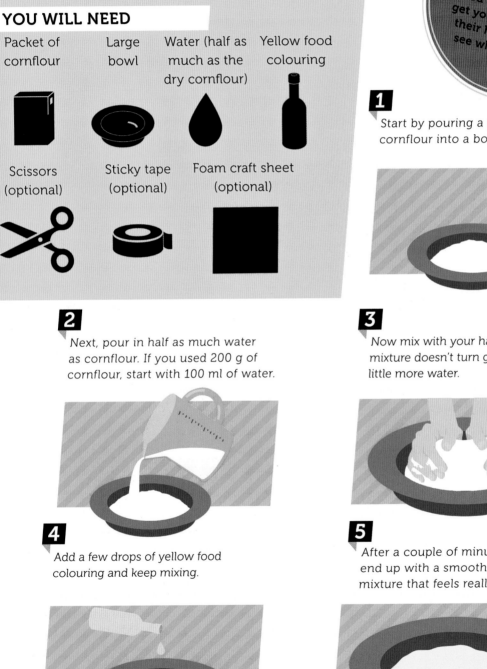

2

Next, pour in half as much water as cornflour. If you used 200 g of cornflour, start with 100 ml of water.

3

Now mix with your hands. If the mixture doesn't turn gloopy, add a little more water.

4

Add a few drops of yellow food colouring and keep mixing.

5

After a couple of minutes, you'll end up with a smooth, sticky mixture that feels really weird!

6

Try this. Dig into the bowl with both hands and shape the goo into a ball. Keep kneading and it'll stay solid...

7

...but as soon as you stop working it, it'll turn into liquid and dribble through your hands into the bowl. Amazing!

> To hide your quicksand in long grass, cut a long, spiky strip of craft foam and tape it around your bowl. Explorers beware!

THE SCIENCE:
VISCOSITY

Viscosity describes how thick and sticky a liquid is. Water is not very viscous, but treacle is. Normally gooey stuff is either more a solid or a liquid, but your goo can switch between the two depending on how much **pressure** it's put under. That's why, as long as you keep kneading it, you can roll it into a ball, but as soon as you stop, it turns back into a liquid.

Bug-O-Scope

Ever wanted to spy on bugs, but find they keep scuttling away?
The Bug-O-Scope will change all that!

YOU WILL NEED

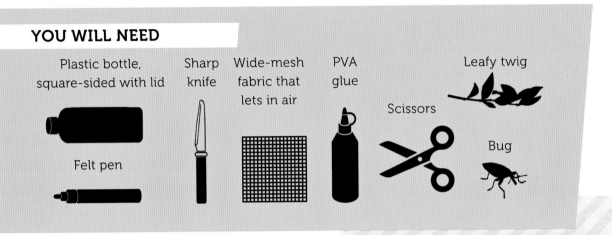

Plastic bottle, square-sided with lid

Felt pen

Sharp knife

Wide-mesh fabric that lets in air

PVA glue

Scissors

Leafy twig

Bug

1
Wash the bottle and dry it well. Draw a rectangle on the top, and ask an adult to cut it out with a sharp knife.

2
Cut a piece of wide-mesh fabric to cover the hole and glue it on.

3
Pop a few leafy twigs into the bottle, then carefully collect a bug and put it in too. Screw the lid on and you have your very own Bug-O-Scope.

THE SCIENCE:
OBSERVATION

Observation, together with recording what you see, is one of the most important parts of science. By observing the way a bug goes about its day, you can test **theories** or ideas against what happens in real life.

After a few hours, return the bug to where you found it and find a different bug to study.

Rain Ruler

Want to know how much rain is falling?
You, my friend, need a rain ruler!

YOU WILL NEED

Plastic bottle

Scissors

Jelly

Bowl

Hot water

Paper clips

Ruler

Permanent pens

1

Carefully cut off the top quarter of a plastic bottle with scissors – ask an adult to start the cut.

2

Make a jelly solution following the packet's instructions. Pour in enough to cover the uneven bottom of the bottle and leave it to set.

3

Turn the top part of the bottle upside down and push it into the bottom part. Use paper clips to hold the two rims together.

4

Hold a ruler against the bottle, lining up the zero with the top of the jelly. Draw on the scales. Put your rain gauge outside where it can't blow over, but don't leave jelly in the rain for too long or it will dissolve!

When the jelly sets, it makes a flat surface inside the bottle so you can measure the rainfall more accurately. Instead of jelly, you could pour in water up to the bottom of the scale.

THE SCIENCE: MEASURING AND PREDICTING

There's a big difference between hearing a weather forecaster say "5 cm of rain fell overnight" and actually measuring it for yourself. Measuring and recording rainfall each day for a long period makes it easier to **predict** weather patterns in the future.

Amazing Avocado

Did you know that it's possible to grow a plant that doesn't need any soil to get started? Meet the amazing avocado!

YOU WILL NEED

Ripe avocado

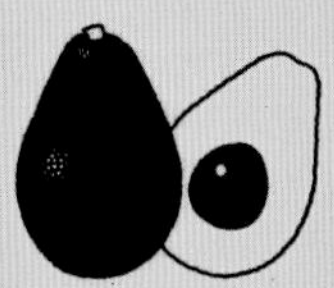

Sharp knife

Glass of water

Three toothpicks

Pot of soil

Sunny spot

Patience

1

Ask an adult to cut an avocado in half carefully so as not to damage the stone or pit inside.

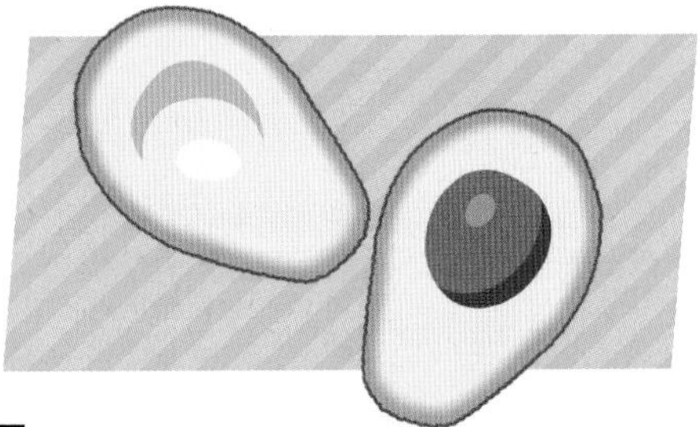

2

Remove the stone and wash off any fruit, being careful not to damage the brown skin.

3

Find the top of the stone – the slightly more pointed end – and push in three toothpicks.

4

Fill a glass with water, then balance the toothpicks on the rim so that the flatter end of the stone is under the water. Place the glass in a sunny spot.

5

Change the water every five days or so. After about eight weeks, the skin will peel and a root will appear.

6

Roots will continue to emerge, and then a single stalk will grow up from the top of the stone.

7

When the stalk is about 15 cm tall, cut it back to about 7.5 cm; this will encourage your plant to grow.

The toothpicks don't damage the avocado because there's a thick, protective barrier around the seed.

8

When it has re-grown to about 15 cm tall, put it in a pot with some soil. Keep it in a sunny spot and make sure the soil is always damp.

THE SCIENCE:
PLANT NUTRIENTS

Most plants begin life in soil, which provides all the **nutrients** or food they need. Avocado plants can grow without soil for the first few weeks because the thick, protective layer around the seed provides all the nutrients the plant needs.

Blooming Colours

Are you bored of white flowers? Would you prefer rainbow-coloured ones? That's no problem, no problem at all...

YOU WILL NEED

Large bowl of cold water

White flowers – chrysanthemums or carnations

Scissors

Warm water

Glass jars

Food colouring

Sharp knife

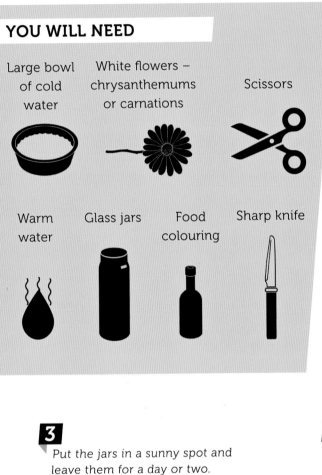

1

Take a bowl and fill it with cold water. Put your flower stems in the water and snip the ends off at a 45-degree angle under the water.

2

Pour a little lukewarm water into the jars. Add drops of food colouring as shown, and pop a flower in each jar.

3

Put the jars in a sunny spot and leave them for a day or two.

4

After a couple of days, the flowers will each be a different colour!

5

Now try this! Take a white flower and ask an adult to carefully cut along the middle of the stem to the end.

6

Put one part of the stem in a jar of water and the other in a jar with water and red food colouring.

7

In two days, the half of the flower in the red water will turn red, while the other half will stay white!

THE SCIENCE:
CAPILLARY ACTION

As water evaporates from the petals, the plant draws water up from the jar to replace it. The way water moves up a plant stem is called capillary action. If you dip the edge of a paper towel in water, you'll see the same thing happen; the water will rise up the paper towel just as it does inside the stem of a plant. The process of moving water from the roots to the leaves and flowers is

Pirate Powerboat

Arrrr, me hearties! Here's how to turn an ordinary plastic bottle into a pirate powerboat.

YOU WILL NEED

Plastic bottle

Square of card

Two plastic straws

Black and white paint

Hand-held drill

Lump of adhesive putty

Sharp pencil

Scissors

White vinegar, about 360 ml

Bowl

Food colouring

Funnel

Baking soda (bicarbonate of soda), 1 tablespoon

1

Paint your bottle, card and one straw black. When the card is dry, paint a skull and crossbones on it.

2

Place one edge of the card on a lump of adhesive putty. Push the tip of a sharp pencil through the centre line of the card into the putty to make a hole. Repeat at the opposite end of the card.

3

Push the straw in through one hole and out through the other. Attach the mast to the boat with adhesive putty.

After step 3, float your boat on some water to check that it's stable. If it isn't, try putting some small stones or marbles inside to give it some extra weight. Give the boat a gentle shake to spread them evenly across the bottom, then float it again.

4

Drill a hole through the bottletop (ask an adult to help). The hole should be just big enough for the other straw to fit through.

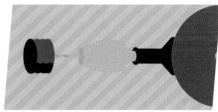

5

Cut the straw in half and push one piece through the hole in the bottletop.

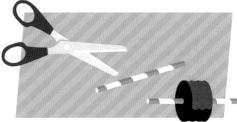

CONTINUED...

6

Pack some adhesive putty around the hole in the bottletop, inside and out, so no air can escape.

7

Next, put the white vinegar in a bowl and stir in about six drops of food colouring.

8

Pop the funnel into the bottle and pour in the vinegar mixture.

9

Fill the bath about one-third full of water, then pop the funnel back in the bottle and add a tablespoon of baking soda.

10

Quickly screw the top (with straw) back on and place your boat in the water. Watch it whoosh away!

Sir Isaac Newton (1643–1727) was an English scientist and mathematician. He is most famous for discovering the laws of gravity and motion.

THE SCIENCE: NEWTON'S LAW OF MOTION

Newton's famous third law says that "for every action there must be an equal and opposite reaction". The vinegar and baking soda react to form carbon dioxide, which makes loads of bubbles that shoot out of the boat. The bubbles push the water backwards, and this makes the boat move forwards (the opposite reaction).

Floating Circle

This fantastical optical illusion makes it look as though the circle is actually moving across the drawing behind it.

It doesn't matter where you start to colour in your rectangles, so long as each one is three squares long, except at the circle's edge.

YOU WILL NEED

Squared graph paper

Pencil

Black felt-tip pen

Sticky tape (to draw around)

Rubber

Lots of patience

!

1

Place your roll of sticky tape in the middle of the graph paper and draw round it lightly in pencil. Then use the felt-tip pen to colour in rectangles, three squares long where possible, inside the circle. At the edge of the circle, just colour in as much of each rectangle as you can.

2

When you've filled the circle, colour in the rectangles surrounding it. Then rub out the pencil circle.

3

And here's what the finished drawing looks like. See how the circle seems to float above the rest of the paper?

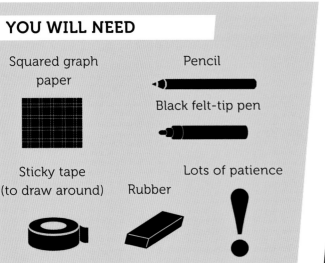

THE SCIENCE: THE OUCHI ILLUSION

This illusion is named after Japanese artist Hajime Ouchi, who invented it. The combination of vertical rectangles and horizontal ones confuses your brain into thinking the circle is floating above the paper. The illusion is stronger if you look at the circle out of the corner of your eye or move your head from side to side.

Magnetic Train

Here's how to build a very simple working magnetic train that flies through a tunnel at breakneck speed.

Warning: these magnets are very strong – adult supervision is needed. Do not place the magnets near mobile phones or computers; they can make them go haywire!

YOU WILL NEED

Pure copper wire (not coated), between 16 and 20 gauge, 6 metres

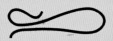

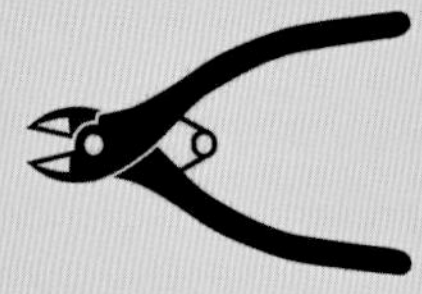

Wire cutters

Marker pen

Six or eight small, disc-shaped neodymium magnets

AAA alkaline battery

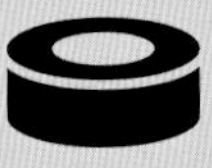

1

Start with a little experiment. Cut off about 2 m of copper wire and wrap it around a marker pen.

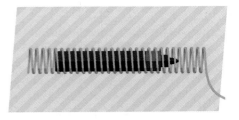

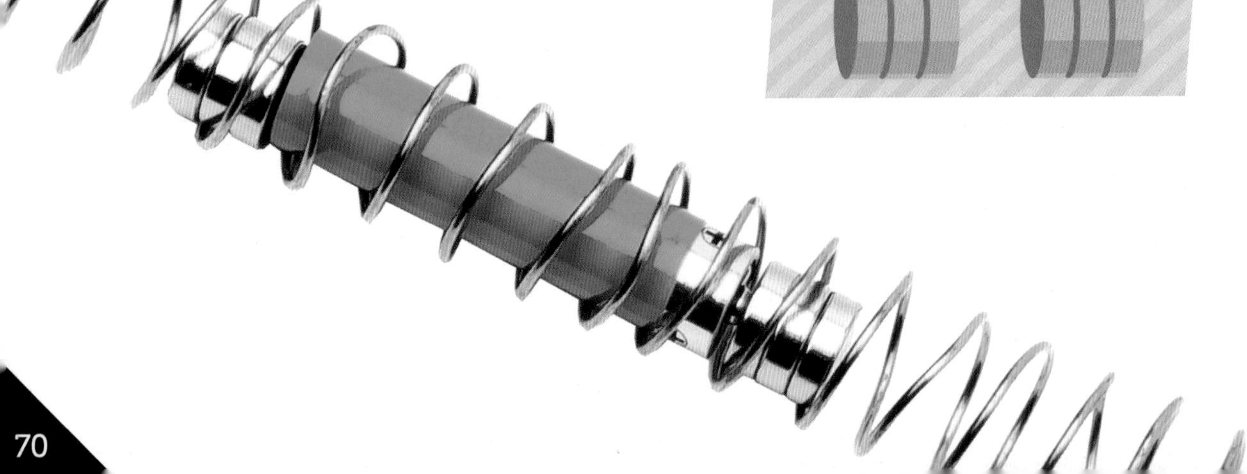

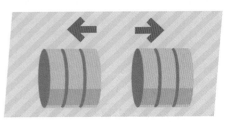

2

Keep going until you've made a short tube about 20 cm long. Cut the end of the wire and remove the marker pen from the tube.

3

Next, let three or four of your disc magnets click together. Repeat, so you have two piles with the same number of magnets. Now position the piles so you can feel them repelling each other.

4

Let the two stacks click into position at either end of the AAA alkaline battery.

5

Push the 'train' into one end of the copper tube. After a second, it will move through the tunnel.

6

Right, that was the experiment! Now take the rest of your copper wire (about 4 m) and make a really long tunnel. Pop the train in one end.

7

As the train shoots off, pull the two ends of the tunnel together.

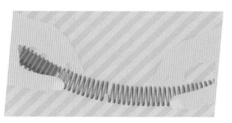

8

The train will now speed through the tunnel until you let it shoot out!

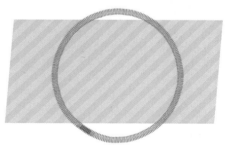

THE SCIENCE:
MAGNETIC FIELDS

The magnets that you add to the battery create a magnet with similar poles at either end: either two north poles or two south poles. The magnets at either end touch the copper wire and create an **electrical circuit**. As electricity flows around the circuit, it creates a magnetic field around the wire. This magnetic field interacts with the magnetic field created by the 'train' in such a way that it pushes the magnets at the back of the train and pulls the ones at the front, moving the train along. The train can only move in one direction.

CD Hovercraft

Here's how you can build a simple hovercraft that uses compressed air to lift itself off the ground and float along above a hard, flat surface – all by itself!

YOU WILL NEED

Water bottle with a pull-up (sports) cap

PVA glue

Old CD

Balloon

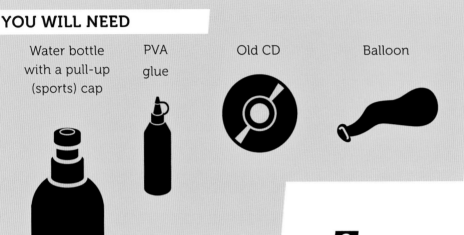

1
Take the cap off the water bottle and put PVA glue around the bottom rim.

2
Check the cap is closed, then press it onto the centre of the CD and give it a twist to make sure no air can get out. Leave the glue to dry.

3
This is the tricky part (you may need adult help). Blow up a balloon, give the end a few twists, open the end and pull it over the top of the bottle cap.

4
Find a flat, hard surface (carpet won't work) and carefully open the bottle cap by pulling it up.

The bigger the balloon, the more air there is inside and the further your hovercraft will fly.

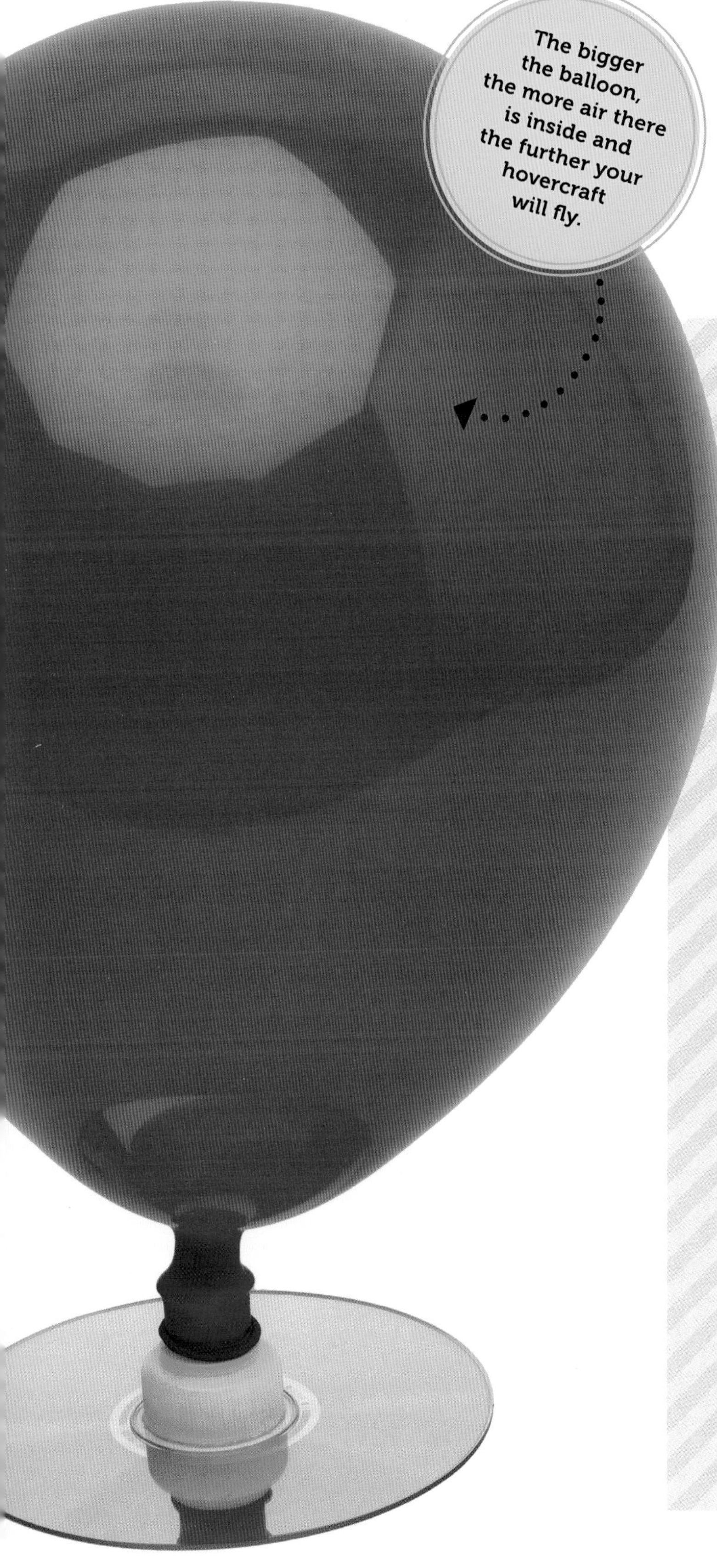

5

Place the hovercraft on a flat surface as quickly as you can and watch it glide away!

THE SCIENCE: AIR AND FRICTION

As air is pushed out of the balloon, it goes down through the hole in the bottle cap, through the hole in the CD and then escapes in all directions, lifting the CD off the surface. This little cushion of air cuts down the **friction** between the CD and the flat surface, and allows it to hover in the air. A gentle nudge with your finger will move it in any direction you like.

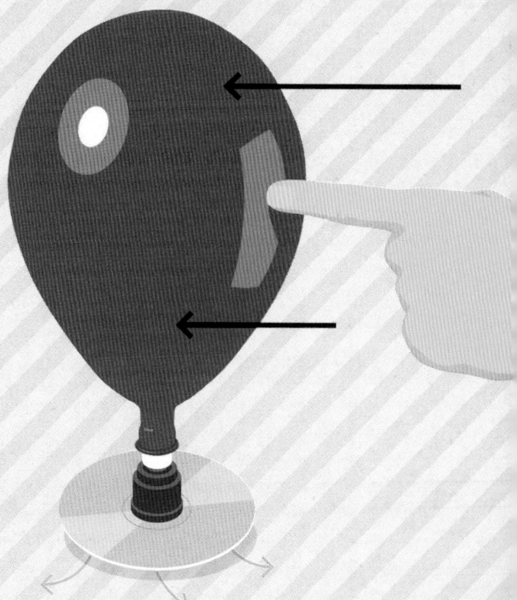

Candypult

Meet the catapult that throws sweets through the air – and teaches you about energy transfer at the same time!

YOU WILL NEED

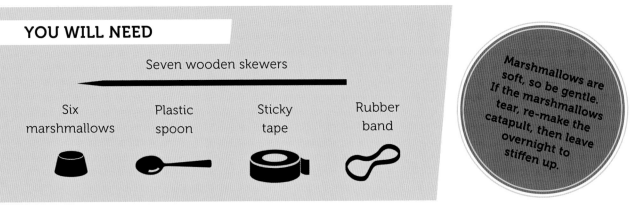

Seven wooden skewers

Six marshmallows

Plastic spoon

Sticky tape

Rubber band

Marshmallows are soft, so be gentle. If the marshmallows tear, re-make the catapult, then leave overnight to stiffen up.

1

Start by taking three marshmallows and position them on a flat surface in a large triangle shape.

2

Take three of the wooden skewers and carefully poke them into each of the marshmallows, as shown.

3

To make the top of the pyramid, hold a fourth marshmallow centrally above the other three and push two more skewers into place.

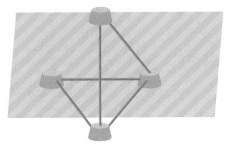

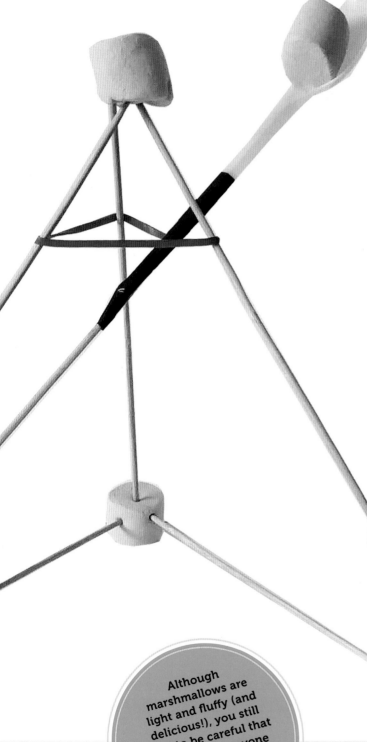

4

Finish off the pyramid by adding a sixth skewer so you have a 3-D triangle with a marshmallow at each corner.

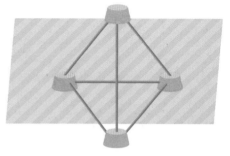

5

Take the final skewer, overlap one end of it with the handle of a plastic spoon and tape the two together.

Although marshmallows are light and fluffy (and delicious!), you still need to be careful that you don't hit anyone when you're firing your catapult. So, look twice, fire once!

CONTINUED...

6

Wrap the tape around several times so the spoon can't fly off!

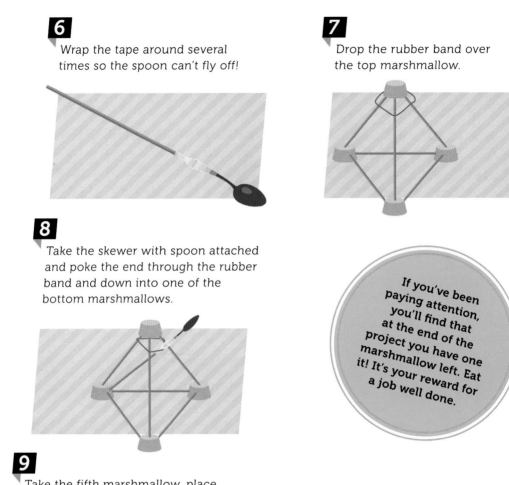

7

Drop the rubber band over the top marshmallow.

8

Take the skewer with spoon attached and poke the end through the rubber band and down into one of the bottom marshmallows.

If you've been paying attention, you'll find that at the end of the project you have one marshmallow left. Eat it! It's your reward for a job well done.

9

Take the fifth marshmallow, place it in the spoon and then, holding the structure with your other hand, pull down on the spoon to stretch the rubber band. When the band is stretched tight, let go and the marshmallow will fly through the air!

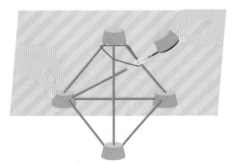

THE SCIENCE:
ENERGY TRANSFER

When you pull back the rubber band, you transfer energy to it. The rubber band stores the energy until you let go of it. Once you let go, the rubber band transfers energy to the marshmallow to make it fly through the air.

Hopalong Frog

Frogs love to jump, right? What happens when they're tired though? Maybe they need a little helping hand...

YOU WILL NEED

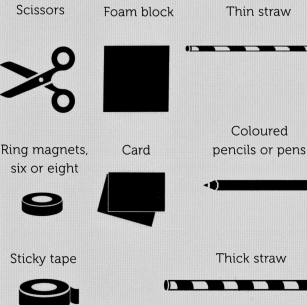

Scissors

Foam block

Thin straw

Ring magnets, six or eight

Card

Coloured pencils or pens

Sticky tape

Thick straw

> **Warning:** these magnets are very strong; adult supervision is needed.

1
Using scissors, poke a hole in the foam block; make the hole just big enough to hold the thin straw.

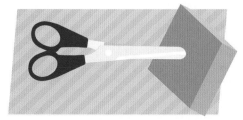

CONTINUED...

2

Next, pop the thin straw into the hole you just made.

3

Take your ring magnets and drop them over the straw so they sit at the bottom.

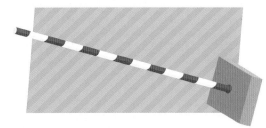

4

Leave a couple of magnets at the bottom and pull the rest of them up and off the end of the straw.

5

Turn the magnets over and drop them back onto the straw. They'll hover above the magnets at the bottom.

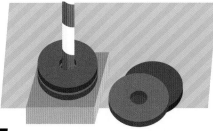

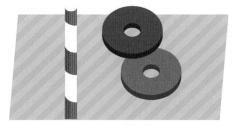

6

Repeat until the magnets are spread out up the straw, with each magnet repelling the one next to it.

7

Take your card and pens or pencils and draw a cheeky frog. Colour it in and then cut it out.

If you're not so fond of frogs, you can draw anything that jumps, such as a grasshopper, a kangaroo or even a Mexican jumping bean!

Can you make the frog jump so high that it comes off the top of the straw? Try adding more magnets to see if you can.

8

Cut a short length off the thick straw and use sticky tape to attach it to the back of the frog.

9

Slide the frog's thick straw onto the thin straw.

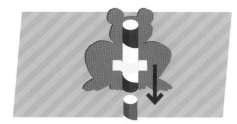

10

Push the frog down so that all the magnets are touching, then let go. Your frog will jump right up to the top of the straw!

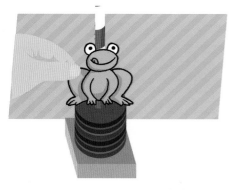

THE SCIENCE:
MAGNETISM

Magnets create invisible magnetic fields that either attract other magnets or push them away (repel them). The north pole of one magnet will attract the south pole of another magnet, but if you turn the second magnet round so that the two north poles are facing each other, the magnetic field will push the magnets apart. By turning the ring magnets around so they repel each other, you create a sort of magnetic spring that makes the frog jump up.

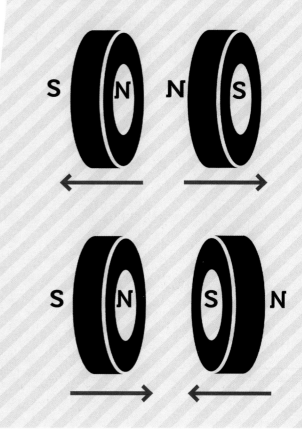

Bottle Diver

How can you make a diver go up and down inside a bottle without touching it? Find out by making this cool bottle diver!

1

Cut this shape from a foam craft sheet, making sure the straight edge is long enough to wrap all the way around the felt-tip pen lid. Wrap it around and glue it in place.

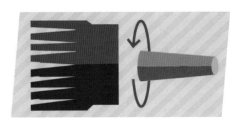

YOU WILL NEED

Foam craft sheet

Scissors

Felt-tip pen lid

Glue

Lump of adhesive putty

Clear plastic bottle (1 litre)

Water

Pair of googly eyes

2

Roll your adhesive putty and stick it around the diver's 'waist'. Add a pair of googly eyes.

3

Remove any labels from the bottle and fill it with water. Then carefully lower the diver into the water.

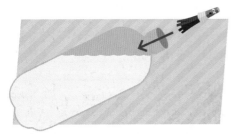

4

Screw on the cap and give the bottle a squeeze. Your diver should descend to the bottom. If it doesn't, add a little more adhesive putty!

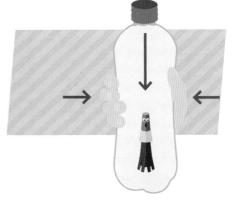

5

Now, stop squeezing the bottle and watch what happens. After a second, the diver will rise to the top!

Scientists call this experiment the Cartesian Diver. 'Cartesian' comes from the name Descartes. René Descartes (1596–1650) was the French scientist who invented it.

THE SCIENCE:
BUOYANCY

When you squeeze the bottle, the little bit of air that's trapped inside the pen cap gets squashed and becomes denser than the water surrounding it. When that happens, it causes the pen cap to sink slowly to the bottom. When you stop squeezing, the little bit of air expands again, forcing water out of the cap and making the diver more **buoyant**, so it rises back up to the top.

Rubber Band Car

Everyone likes fast cars, right? Now you can build one of your very own, powered just by rubber bands!

YOU WILL NEED

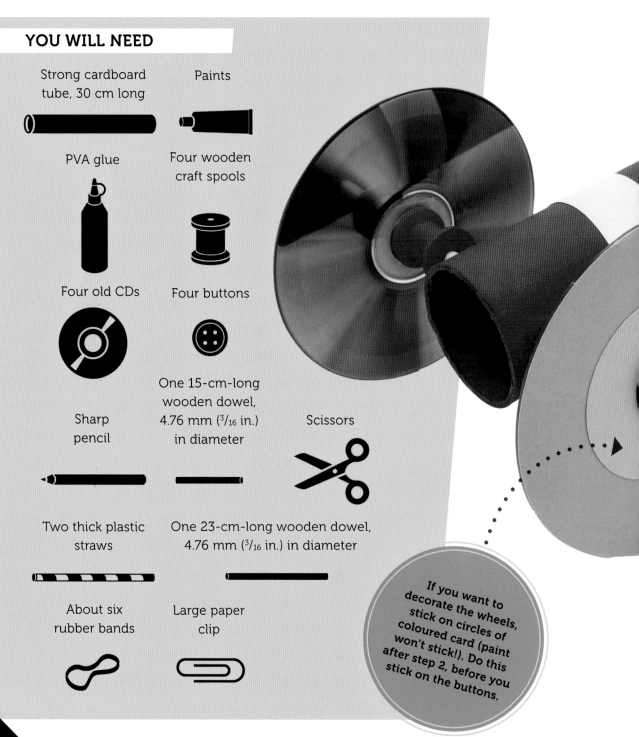

Strong cardboard tube, 30 cm long

Paints

PVA glue

Four wooden craft spools

Four old CDs

Four buttons

Sharp pencil

One 15-cm-long wooden dowel, 4.76 mm (³/₁₆ in.) in diameter

Scissors

Two thick plastic straws

One 23-cm-long wooden dowel, 4.76 mm (³/₁₆ in.) in diameter

About six rubber bands

Large paper clip

If you want to decorate the wheels, stick on circles of coloured card (paint won't stick!). Do this after step 2, before you stick on the buttons.

1

Start by painting the cardboard tube (the car's body). You could even give it a number, like a racing car.

If your car's wheels don't grip too well, you could try wrapping a few rubber bands across the CDs. These will act like tyres and give the wheels more grip.

2

Next, use PVA glue to stick a wooden spool to the centre of each CD.

3

When they're dry, flip the CDs over and glue a button to the centre of each one – these are the hubcaps.

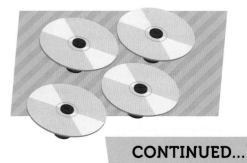

CONTINUED...

4

Use a sharp pencil to make a hole about 2.5 cm in from one end of the cardboard tube.

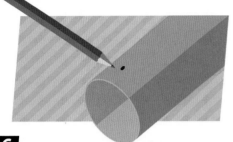

5

Make another hole opposite the first one. Poke the shorter dowel through both holes to make the front axle.

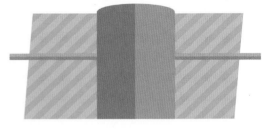

6

Cut two short lengths from one of the thick drinking straws and slide them onto the axle, as shown.

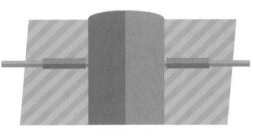

7

Slide on the wheels and check that both wheels turn freely.

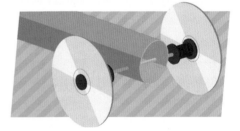

8

Take the wheels off and squeeze some glue into each spool hole. Pop the wheels back onto the axle.

9

To make the rear wheels, repeat steps 4 to 8 but use the longer dowel and longer lengths of straw.

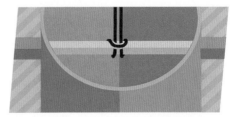

10

Next, loop six rubber bands together like this to make a chain of rubber bands.

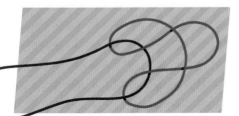

11

Loop the end rubber band around the front axle, as shown.

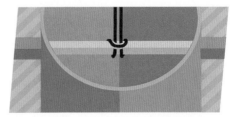

12

Attach the paper clip to the other end of the rubber band chain and drop it through the tube.

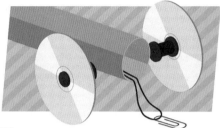

13

Clip the paper clip to the end of the tube by the rear wheels.

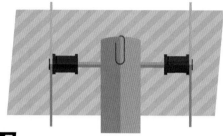

14

To wind up the car, turn the front wheels anti-clockwise to wrap the rubber bands around the front axle.

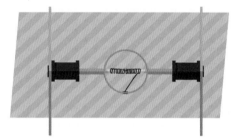

15

When the rubber bands are tight, put the car on the ground and let go!

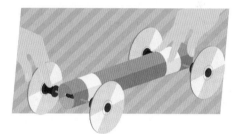

THE SCIENCE:
ENERGY STORES

When you wrap the rubber band around the axle, you transfer energy to the rubber band as it stretches. The band increases its potential energy store; that's energy stored up ready to use later. When you release the wheels, the rubber band returns to its natural, unstretched shape, and transfers its stored energy to the car, making it move.

Wingless Plane

You might think that a plane with no wings wouldn't fly very far. Just wait till you meet this wingless glider; it'll fly much further than ordinary paper planes!

YOU WILL NEED

Ruler

Pencil

Sheet of card

Scissors

Sticky tape

Paper straw

1
Using a ruler and pencil, draw two strips about 2.5 cm wide on a sheet of card – make one strip about half as long as the other – and cut them out.

2
Bend the strips of card over to make hoops and secure them with sticky tape.

3
Tape the hoops to the straw, as shown.

4
Throw the plane into the air with the smaller hoop facing forwards.

THE SCIENCE:
LIFT

The hoops act just like wings. When you throw the plane, the air flows around the hoops and creates lift: the force that pushes the plane up. The big hoop also creates drag, which keeps the plane level, while the small one prevents it from turning, so it flies further.

If you think the plane is not flying as far as it could, poke a paper clip onto the end of the straw with the small hoop and throw again.

Fish in a Bowl

Here's a clever way to make it look as though a fish is inside a fishbowl, even when you know it isn't!

To make sure you draw them in the right place, imagine the two drawings on top of each other.

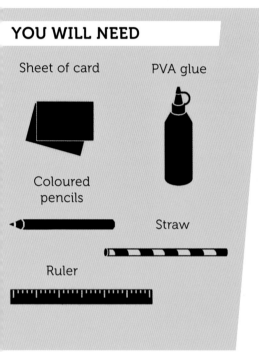

YOU WILL NEED

Sheet of card

PVA glue

Coloured pencils

Straw

Ruler

1
Fold your rectangle of card in half so the two short edges meet. Draw an empty fishbowl on the front and a fish on the back. Make sure they are the same way up!

2
Open up the card and, on the inside, use a ruler and pencil to measure and mark the vertical centre line. Stick the top of the straw along the line. Then put glue around the edges of the card and stick them together. Leave to dry.

3
Hold the straw between the palms of your hands and roll it backwards and forwards. As the card spins, the fish will appear inside the fishbowl, as if by magic!

THE SCIENCE: STICKY FISH

When you see something – such as the fish or the bowl – and then look away, the image 'sticks' in your eye for about one-tenth of a second; this is called 'persistence of vision'. As you spin the card toy (called a thaumatrope), the 'stickiness' blends the two images into one so it looks as if the fish is actually inside the bowl.

Vanishing Rainbow

It's exciting to see a rainbow, but here we're going to show you how to make one disappear!

YOU WILL NEED

Coloured crayons

White card

Scissors

Ruler

Wooden skewer

Lump of adhesive putty

1
Draw a circle on a sheet of white card and cut it out. With the help of a ruler, draw eight sections on the disc, like the slices of a pie.

2
Colour the sections in this order: red, orange, yellow, green, blue, **indigo** and violet. Leave the last section white.

3
Put a lump of adhesive putty on a table, then place the centre of the card disc on the putty. Poke a wooden skewer through the centre into the putty to make a hole.

4
Wiggle the skewer to make the hole slightly larger, then spin the disc on the skewer. The colours will disappear and all you'll see is greyish-white. The rainbow has vanished!

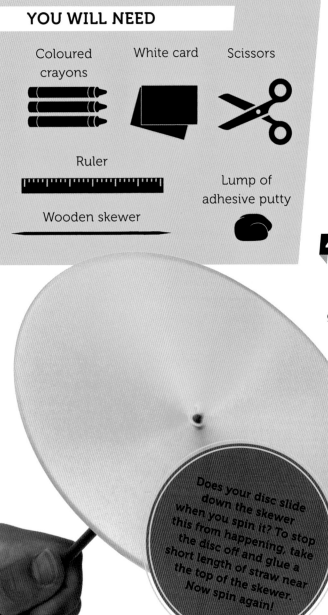

Does your disc slide down the skewer when you spin it? To stop this from happening, take the disc off and glue a short length of straw near the top of the skewer. Now spin again!

THE SCIENCE: LIGHT AND COLOUR

White light is a combination of all the other colours that we can see (the **visible spectrum**). When you spin the wheel fast, your eyes can't distinguish the separate colours. What they see is all the colours blended to a greyish-white.

Spiral Mobile

Watch as this marvellous mobile twists and turns
like a snake in the air – all by itself!

YOU WILL NEED

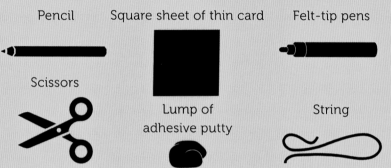

Pencil

Square sheet of thin card

Felt-tip pens

Scissors

Lump of
adhesive putty

String

1

Draw a small circle in the middle of the card, then draw
a spiral around it. Keep drawing until the spiral fills the
card, then use felt-tip pens to decorate your spiral.

2

Carefully cut out the spiral. Cut all the way along
the line until you reach the start of your spiral.

3

Make a small hole in the centre of your mobile by placing it on
a lump of adhesive putty and pushing the tip of a sharp pencil
through the circle into the putty. Tie a knot at the end of a length
of string and thread the other end through the hole. Ask an adult
to hang your mobile above a heater. Watch what happens!

THE SCIENCE:
THE HEAT GOES UP

Hot air is lighter than colder air and rises upwards. A heater
heats up the air above it. As the hot air rises, it pushes on
the spiral's sloping card and makes it spin around.

Move the
spiral away from
the heater and let
it settle. It won't
move because
there's no warm
air pushing it.

Exploding Ninja Stick Bomb

OK, this isn't really a bomb and these sticks aren't really going to explode; but it's a neat trick and a great demonstration of a chain reaction.

YOU WILL NEED

Five craft sticks (or lollipop sticks)

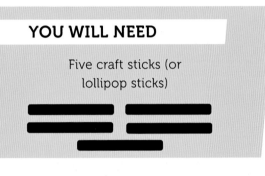

 1

Start by making a 'V' shape like this, with one stick overlapping the other at the bottom of the 'V'.

2

Place a third stick on top of the first two, like this.

3

Holding the shape at the bottom, insert the next stick, as shown.

4

Slide the stick you just inserted down a little and weave the final stick over and under, as shown.

5

And here's the finished 'bomb' ready to be exploded.

6

Drop the bomb onto a hard floor, such as tiles. When it hits, the sticks will fly off in all directions.

THE SCIENCE:
CHAIN REACTION

As you weave the sticks together, you can feel them straining against your fingers and against each other. As soon as the 'bomb' hits something, the balance is broken and the sticks fly apart as they return to their natural state: straight, and not under tension. This is an example of a chain reaction, where one stick affects the next, which affects the next, and so on.

You can make much more complicated Ninja stick bombs than this one. Try searching online for 'cobra weave stick bomb'. These patterns use hundreds of sticks in one bomb!

Unbreakable Egg

Using just a few straws and some sticky tape, here's how to drop an uncooked egg from a great height without breaking it!

YOU WILL NEED

2 strong plastic straws (e.g. red)

12 strong plastic straws (e.g. blue)

Raw egg

Wide sticky tape

Scissors

1

Cut one of the red straws into three pieces, each slightly longer than the egg. Repeat with the other red straw.

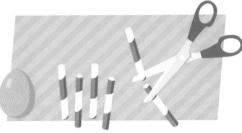

2

Tape the six pieces of straw into a pyramid shape, then slip the egg into the middle. It should sit securely.

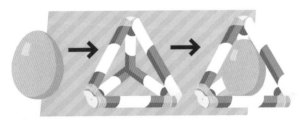

3

Now tape two of the blue straws together to make one long straw. Repeat until you have six of these.

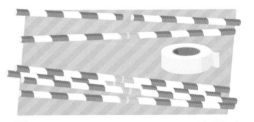

4

Tape one of these long blue straws parallel to one of the red straws that make up the central pyramid.

5

Repeat on one of the other sides, as shown.

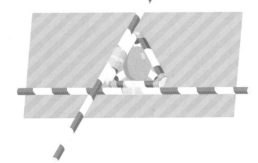

6

Continue until you've attached all six of the super-long straws to the short straws.

7

Take your contraption outside to a high place and drop it. If you've built it right, your egg should survive intact!

THE SCIENCE: FORCE PATHS

The reason this project works is simple: none of the straws are pointing at the egg. So no matter which way up your contraption lands, the force of the impact will travel up the straws and past the egg. If you were to have straws pointing at the egg, they would almost certainly puncture the shell as the contraption hit the ground.

See how many times you can drop your contraption without breaking the egg.

Glossary

While we've done our best to explain various scientific principles as they apply to the different 'makes' in the book, there may be one or two you're still not sure about.

3-D
Short for three-dimensional. A drawing on paper has two dimensions – width and height – but by adding shadows and perspective you can give it depth, which creates the illusion of a third dimension.

Acids (and alkalis)
An acid is a substance that reacts strongly with some metals and tastes sour. Lemons contain citric acid, which is why they taste sour. Acids can be neutralised by substances called alkalis, which dissolve in water.

Amplify
To increase the volume of a sound so that it becomes louder. One way to do this is to focus the sound; that's why cupping your hands around your mouth lets you shout more loudly.

Bacteria
Tiny organisms made up of a single cell that can be troublemakers. Bacteria can give you a sore throat, for example.

Binary
Something that's made up of only two things, for example a zero and a one, or a switch that can only be turned on or off.

Buoyant
Something that floats is buoyant. It is caused to float by an upward force called buoyancy.

Buttermilk
The tangy liquid that is left over once you've churned butter.

Carbon
A chemical element that it is in everything – seriously! Everyone reading this book is 18 per cent carbon!

Chemical element
A pure substance that only contains one type of atom.

Condense
When a gas gets cooler and then turns into a liquid. For example, on a hot day moisture in the air condenses as water droplets on the outside of a cold can of fizzy drink from the fridge.

Constellation
A collection of stars that form a pattern. The pattern usually refers to an Earthly object (such as a plough) or a figure from myth (such as Pegasus, the horse with wings).

Electrical circuit
The path around which an electric current flows and transfers energy.

Energy
The ability to do stuff. For example, food provides us with the energy we need to keep warm, move and talk. Batteries provide energy to make electrical circuits work.

Evaporate
What happens when you apply heat to a liquid and it turns into a gas. Leave a cold can of fizzy drink to warm up and the droplets of condensation on the can will evaporate into the air, leaving the can dry.

Force
The effect that one object can have on another object. A force can either be a push or a pull.

Frequency
The number of sound vibrations that occur every second.

Friction

The resistance that happens when one object rubs across the surface of another. Try rolling a toy car across a wood floor and then across a carpet to see the difference in friction.

Geometry

The study of shapes and how they fit together.

Indigo

A colour that is a cross between blue and violet.

Magnetic field

The region around a magnet where magnetic forces can attract or repel anything made of a magnetic material.

Mass

Mass is the amount of matter that makes a particular object. Every object in the universe has mass. Although it's usually measured in units of weight, it's not the same as weight, which is a force: how much a mass is pulled by Earth's gravity.

Matter

Anything that has mass and takes up space is made of matter. You're made of matter. So is this book.

Molecules

A group of atoms that are bound together chemically.

Nutrients

Essential substances for plants and animals to live and grow. Nutrients such as food provide us with energy. Nutrients such as minerals from the soil help plants to grow healthily.

Oxidation

The chemical reaction that happens when a substance reacts with oxygen. When iron is exposed to oxygen, it rusts.

Particles

Very tiny particles of matter.

Pitch

When you hear a series of musical notes and can tell which ones are high and which ones are low, you are listening to their pitch. Pitch is the result of sound waves vibrating at different frequencies.

Plasticizer

Something that is added to a substance to make it more flexible and less brittle.

Predict

To make a scientific guess about what will happen in the future based on observations of what has happened in the past.

Pressure

A force on an object that acts over an area; for example, air acting on the sides of a balloon or water acting on the sides of a container.

Resonate

The way a noise sounds for longer by reflecting from a surface or by causing nearby objects to vibrate. Try shouting in a completely empty room and your voice will resonate.

Theories

Ways of explaining things that happen, supported by observations and experiments. Some theories have been formed without any actual proof at all.

Vibrations

The shaking of particles that go to make up an object. For example, twanging a ruler or elastic band makes it vibrate.

Visible spectrum

This is all the stuff we can see, such as light. There's also an electromagnetic spectrum, which is full of stuff we can't see, such as ultraviolet light and radio waves.

Index